CLEAN

ORGANIC HOUSEHOLD TIPS
THAT DON'T COST THE EARTH

Stephanie Zia

Blackbird Digital Books
London

REVISED, RETITLED AND UPDATED FEBRUARY 2020

Blackbird Digital Books 2011
First published as an ebook, *'Done & Dusted – The Organic Home on a Budget'*
March 2010
© Stephanie Zia 2011. All rights reserved
ISBN-13: 978-1916426887
COVER IMAGE: bogitw/679 Pixabay

All prices quoted are liable to fluctuation and change at any time. It is the reader's responsibility to check with each individual supplier whether taxes, postage and packing are included before placing any orders.

For Jennie Trisnan

WHAT READERS ARE SAYING

'I admit to being the worst house-cleaner of anybody who has ever lived. I hate housework. But not any more! This book has CHANGED MY LIFE! BRILLIANT book. It should be required reading for every housewife/househusband.' NoDamnBlog

'I was partly expecting it to be yet another 'lemons and white wine vinegar' kind of book, but it's actually full of interesting new ideas and products.' Penny GoLightly

'I LOVE IT!! The writing style is so readable and no nonsense. I used the cleaning method described in chapter 1 a long time ago but never used it properly. The book is fantastic.' Deborah McDonnell, BA, BSc (Hons), MCPP Holistic Herbal

'Jam-packed full of startling facts about how much damage we are potentially doing to the environment simply via our choice of cleaning products.' The School Run Website

Contents

C1 Stain Removal Without A Chart, The Knowledge p1

C2 The Housework Hater's Healthy Quick Cleaning Guide p10

C3 What About the Vinegar? p19

C4 Toxic Chemicals in the Home p32

C5 How to Make Healthy Home-made Air Fresheners p41

C6 The Cheapest Way To Double Your Storage Space p43

C7 The Humane Way to Get Rid of Rats, Mice & Ants p45

C8 A Healthy Kitchen p47

C9 Why Optical Brighteners are Optical Illusions – 30 Degree EcoWashing p57

C10 A Little Bit of Dirt... What's Wrong With Chemical Anti-Bacterials? p61

C11 A Healthy Bathroom p63

C12 Are You Getting The Most Out of Your Household Contents Insurance? p74

C13 Help! 100+ Readers' Cleaning and Stains Catastrophes Solved p76

Links p153

Introduction

Welcome to my practical cleaning and lifestyle tip miscellany, designed to help you reduce your toxic chemical footprint on your body, your home and the planet without breaking the budget.

This book is not anti-chemical – everything is made of chemicals – but about balance. How to use organic wherever possible and avoid the known and possible dangers and make informed, affordable compromises.

Avoiding the nasties lurking in the products we regularly use for cleaning, laundering and 'refreshing' the air isn't as straightforward as looking at the labels. Consumer information is shockingly vague. Until recently manufacturers were under no obligation at all to reveal what was in their products, often citing trade secrets. Things are changing, but very slowly. Certain issues, like the widespread use of toxic, banned, flame retardants which pollute our homes and poison the air when fires do occur, are still very much in the news in 2020.

In the US, organisations like *Safer Chemicals, Healthy Families* and *Women's Voices for the Earth* have a tough job on their hands persuading Congress to change their policies in the face of powerful corporate opposition. In Europe, progress has been faster. All the provisions set out in the European Union REACH chemical regulation agreement were finally put in place in 2018 and can be found online in *The REACH Handbook*, the complete guide to substance of very high concern (SVHC).

At the end of the day, it's down to you and hopefully this book will help. Where there are areas of confusion and controversy – the question of chemicals leaching from plastic bottles, for example, or whether we should be avoiding non-stick pans – links to carefully researched, non-alarmist, websites are recommended to help you make up your own mind.

Stephanie

CHAPTER ONE

Stain Removal Without a Chart – The Knowledge

Shortly after my A – Z of stain removal *Your Really Useful Guide to Getting Rid of Stains* was published by Hamlyn in 2005 I began writing for Space Solves, *The Guardian*'s Weekend magazine advice column. This book started as a collection of those columns, and gradually grew as I added miscellanies of household tips that I have picked up along the way. I always recommend the healthiest, most ecologically sound method of cleaning and stain removal wherever possible, but only if it works and not solely for the sake of its green credentials. There's no use at all recommending a non-toxic product if it's not going to work. An awareness of the dangers of inhaling, touching and disposing of certain chemicals, acting accordingly and only using them when absolutely necessary is, I believe, the sensible way forward.

Speed is of the essence. The quicker you can wipe up that spill, the easier it's going to be to completely remove it. In this chapter you'll learn how to categorise a stain the instant it happens so that you can treat it confidently and successfully.

There are just 3 main types of stain:
Greasy, Protein, Tannin

Plus 3 smaller sub-categories:
Dye, Combination, Special

1. Greasy Stains *! Don't leave greasy fabrics soaking in hot water for too long. As the water cools the grease particles will redistribute themselves all over the fabric. ! Never iron over a greasy stain or a shadow of a greasy stain or you'll set it permanently.*

Greasy stains come from spills that have grease, oil or fat in them like butter, face cream and engine oil. Greasy stains often aren't as bad as they look and come out easily with HOT water and WASHING-UP LIQUID.

To summarise: You get a SPILL – WAAGH!

Ask yourself, is this a stain that comes from grease or oil?

GREASY STAIN = HOT water & WASHING-UP LIQUID

2. Protein Stains *!Don't treat protein stains with hot water or you could set them permanently.*

Protein stains are the most common group. These are food stains resulting from animal products, like baby formula, eggs, cheese and yoghurt, any stains that come from animals and humans like sweat, sick and excrement or any organic stains that come from the earth which aren't liquid tannin stains like mud, leaf-mould and vegetables. Protein stains come out with

COLD water.

Some stains, especially those resulting from food cooked in oil like curries, are a combination of protein and grease and need a two-step treatment, see *Combination Stains* below.

To summarise:

SPILL – WAAGH! Did it come from a human, animal or directly out of the ground?

PROTEIN STAIN = COLD water & a little washing-up liquid.

3. **Tannin Stains** *! Don't use soap on tannin stains or you'll set them permanently.*

Tannin stains come from direct liquid spills that originate in plants like tea, coffee, alcohol, perfume, fruit juice, herbs and spices.

Tannin stains come out best when treated with HOT water.

BUT

Sugar Tannin eg fermented alcohol and fruit like wine, honey, cola, beer and jam, and **Protein Tannin** eg, tea or coffee with milk added, must be treated with **cold** water. Fast action really makes a difference here as sugar tannin stains are much more likely to come out if they're not allowed to dry out. Use soda water if possible, otherwise, cold water. For carpet stains, use kitchen paper and press it down really hard so that it absorbs the liquid. Keep on changing the paper until the stain has been absorbed. This works really well on immediate wine, tea and coffee spills. For old, dried-in red wine, tea and coffee stains, try Glycerine (about £2/$3.24, from the pharmacy). Dab with cold water and rub the Glycerine in with a finger. You may have to repeat this several times. Or use Borax Substitute. Make a runny paste by mixing a teaspoon of borax with a desert-spoon of hot water. Dribble it over the stain, when it's turned black, sponge off with cool water.

To summarise:

SPILL – WAAGH! Is this a stain that comes from alcohol, or a liquid that comes from a plant?

COULD BE A TANNIN STAIN = HOT water. If it's possible hold the reverse side of the stain under fast-flowing hot running water to flush the stain out through the fibres.

BUT HANG ON! Does it have anything added, like milk in coffee? Sugar in tea? Is the alcohol fermented, like wine? SUGAR TANNIN = COLD water (preferably soda water). If cold water doesn't get it out, move on to borax, Glycerine or Wine Away.

There are a few other, smaller, categories of stain:

4. Dye Stains

The most difficult fruit stains, cherry and blueberry, have dye in them as do those blue ice lollies and ice pops. This category also covers colour runs resulting from washing whites with a colour.

To summarise: SPILL – WAAGH! Does it have dye in it, synthetic or natural like blueberry, cherry or pomegranate?

Dye stains are one area where a commercial stain removal product is worth keeping handy in your store cupboard. One of the best is Wine Away (see *Chapter 3 – What About The Vinegar?*), which can successfully remove all sorts of red stains as well as wine. Natural dye stains like cherry, blueberry and pomegranate stand a much better chance of being removed if they're treated whilst still wet. Add a teaspoon of vinegar to a cup of milk to sour it, saturate the stain and leave for 30 minutes to an hour. Rinse in cool water, agitating the fabric up against itself. Rinse thoroughly or you'll be left with a smelly milk stain. If the spill happens on a hard surface, soak a kitchen towel in sour milk, place over the stain and weigh it down for 30 minutes with something heavy. If felt tip and ink marks are proving impossible to remove, look up the manufacturer online, they may be able to recommend a product. As a last resort you could try going over the mark again with fresh pen. With some types of inks, the liquid will be absorbed by the dry ink, making it fluid again. Cover the stain with a piece of cotton wool soaked in milk and keep replacing until all the ink has been absorbed.

Another method: after colour testing, spot-treat with a cloth dipped in methylated spirits. Better still, mix equal parts of methylated spirits and ammonia together (one of the only times when you can mix ammonia with anything) and dab at the stains. If you're using ammonia, follow all safety instructions, ventilate the room, wear a mask and make sure all children and pets are far away. Rinse thoroughly. DYE = If it's a colour run stain act fast. Don't let it dry out – soak in a bowl of cold water with soda crystals. Go out and buy a colour run remover like Dylon Colour Run Remover.

5. Combination Stains

A few stains are a combination of the above.

Grease and protein: protein foods made with oil or grease like tomato ketchup, gravy, curry, chocolate. As heat sets protein stains, treat with cold water first to get rid of the protein part of the stain and then hot water & washing up liquid to get rid of the grease. If you're left with a nasty shadow of a stain, treat with glycerine.

Grease and wax/dye/oil: these are those tricky mascara, lipstick, shoe polish and tar stains. Some crayons fit into this category. Use Goo Gone, or Graffiti Go if you have it. If not, try WD40 or Methylated Spirits.

6. Special Stains

These are stains that don't fit into any of the above categories:

Anti-perspirant Those pale, powdery underarm marks. White vinegar usually works on fresh stains. Or make a paste of detergent and water and apply to both sides of the stains before laundering. For old marks, dilute ammonia 50/50 with cool water.
Chemical spills Most manufacturers have phone help lines and increasingly more have free live web-chat

facilities. Look for phone number and website address on the packet. Alternatively ask at your hardware store help desk.

Chewing gum Cover with bag of ice. If size permits, wrap in a plastic bag and put the garment in the freezer for a few hours. When the gum is brittle and frozen – break it off.

Grass Grass is technically a protein stain but it's a particularly difficult one. Soak in oxygen bleach. If stains remain dab with white vinegar or methylated spirits.

Nail varnish, lacquer Alternate dabs with a non-oily nail varnish remover and cool water.

Mildew First, brush off the excess, preferably outdoors but certainly not in a confined space. Always wear a mask when you do this because inhaling the tiny mildew spores is very bad for your lungs. Soak in sour milk or apply an antiseptic. TCP is good but the smell does linger. Diluted Tea Tree essential oil is good for small stains like garden chair cushions etc. Rinse milk off in cold water and washing up liquid before it dries.

Pencil Pencil eraser. If stubborn, Magic sponge. For impossibly stubborn marks, ammonia.

Pollen Don't rub. If on fabric, first take outside and shake vigorously. Lift off with sellotape or brush very lightly with a dry toothbrush without applying any pressure. If any marks are left, soak in biological detergent and hot water. If any marks remain, apply neat biological detergent (liquid or make a paste) to both sides of stain and launder in hottest water that's safe for the fabric. If on carpets or non-washable fabrics, spot treat with Isopropyl Alcohol.

Rubber and heel marks Use a pencil eraser or rubber toe of plimsoll. For very stubborn marks try a Magic Eraser Block.

Scorch Rub small marks with the side of a silver coin. Larger marks can be impossible to remove but try soaking in borax/warm water or 3% hydrogen peroxide solution to 4 parts water. Some surface scorch marks on carpets can be removed by carefully snipping the damaged fibre away with a very sharp pair of scissors.

Soot/smoke Biological (enzyme) detergent, WD40 or Magic Eraser Block

Tarnish On metal: tomato ketchup, leave for 10 minutes. On fabric: vinegar or lemon juice.

White Correction Fluid Can be impossible to remove. If on fabric, place in plastic bag in freezer for a few hours and try and pick it off. Dab any marks left with White Spirit.

Tobacco Glycerine or methylated spirits.

Water For water spots on all fabrics apart from silk and chiffon – steam over boiling water. White water marks on wood are caused by trapped moisture – hold a warm hairdryer near the mark, and buff with a cloth. Keep doing this for about 10 to 15 minutes. On non-varnished wooden surfaces, try rubbing with a little non-gel toothpaste. Don't use toothpaste on veneer or it could permanently damage the surface. Toothpaste can lighten some wood. If this happens, restore with Briwax Furniture Reviver or a Briwax Dye Touchup Pen.

Wax Ice method (as for chewing gum). On hard surfaces, melt the wax with a hairdryer and absorb with kitchen towel as it melts. If the wax is on a deep-pile carpet, freeze with ice and pick off as much as you can before melting the wax. Clear up any greasy residue with WD-40, rinse WD-40 off with a little washing-up liquid and thoroughly rinse the carpet. You could also try laying some greaseproof paper over the stain and lightly ironing with a warm iron but beware of having the iron too hot or you could do permanent damage. Treat any residue as greasy stain.

CHAPTER TWO

The Housework Hater's Healthy Quick Cleaning Guide

So, who cleans their house with vinegar? Thought so. Vinegar's a great grease remover but it doesn't scour and, even if disguised with essential oil, that smell does linger.

Bicarbonate of Soda is a brilliant mildly abrasive cleaner, deodoriser and stain remover. But it can permanently bleach colours, and those little tubs of baking soda you get at the supermarket don't go very far do they? Lemons smell wonderful but aren't exactly cheap or practical.

The good news is, as far as day-to-day cleaning goes, you can forget them all. They have plenty of uses, but the only thing you need for speedy, efficient cleaning around the home is a cloth and water.

The E-cloth is the most life-changing, chore-reducing product to appear in the home since the dishwasher. Whether it's the money, health, water and planet-saving or the drudge time-saving aspect that's so amazing about these cloths is a difficult call. Let's start with the obvious.

Money One £5.00 ($8.00) cloth cleans without the need for any chemicals or cleaning products at all. Over a period of 3 years, the potential saving on cleaning products for a small flat would be about £246 ($398).

How does it work? Micro technology. The width of each fibre is 1/100th the size of a human hair and each square centimetre of cloth has 480,000 strands. These fibres and their wedge-shape construction give the cloth its extraordinary cleaning power and its high and rapid absorbency. Unlike a normal cloth which pushes the dirt around and leaves a chemical residue, the hundreds of thousands of tiny micro-hooks lift off and absorb grease, viruses, germs, and grime all by themselves. The cloth cleans all hard surfaces, including thick grease and is ideal for the kitchen and bathroom.

If you want a visible test, start by cleaning a window or a mirror. Fold and spritz a dry cloth or the surface very lightly with a spray bottle of water and wipe across the glass. That's it. Clean, sparkling and smear-free. You'll find you can clean a whole wall of windows, inside and out, in minutes with a better, healthier result (see *Chapter 3 – Toxic Chemicals In the Home* and *Chapter 10 – A Little Bit of Dirt: What's Bad About Chemical Anti-Bacterials)*. If you're using the standard E-cloth rather than the (thinner, finer) Glass and Window Cloth, shake out the cloth before use to ensure no grit from a previous clean has been trapped in the fibres.

Fighting the Superbugs Microfibre cleaning technology was first adopted in Scandinavia, particularly in Norway, during the 1990s to fight hospital superbugs. Using just water, E-cloths are highly effective at removing over 99% of bacteria, including E coli, along with dirt and grease, from domestic surfaces. Because the cloths don't leave any residue on the cleaned surface, there's nothing left behind to encourage the development of bacteria.

Today this cleaning system is widely used throughout Scandinavia – in hospitals, schools and businesses as well as in homes and the word is spreading. Scotland's new high-tech hospital, the Forth Valley Royal, has installed microfibre cleaning robots in its operating theatres, and they're working – MRSA stats are down. The NHS are increasingly introducing microfibre cleaning systems across the UK.

If you want extra freshness, choose the antibacterial E-cloth as your first multi-purpose cloth. The antibacterial element is no relative of the chemical sprays. Here it's a natural nano-silver which kills bacteria caught in the cloth.

Time I resent time spent on housework as much as the next person and, for me, I think this might be the most impressive saving of all. I use E-cloths to clean kitchen surfaces, the hob, the fridge door, walls, tiles, doors, handles, baths, sinks, taps, shower screens, mirrors, windows, furniture (wooden and upholstered), skirting boards, shelves and floors. I also use them to:

• wipe down curtains
• clean inside my car – upholstery, windows, mirrors, interior doors and dash
• clean upholstery and clothes. They're excellent for dry-clean only coats, dresses and soft furnishings that only need a bit of a freshening up.

• as a quick carpet cleaner when I can't be bothered to get the vacuum out. A quick mid-week wipe over the floor around the sofa, dining table and fireplace is a very effective use of 5 minutes a week.

Do's and don'ts

• Don't use soaking wet. The less water the stronger the microfibres can grip.

• Don't be tempted to use with any cleaning products. They'll obstruct the power of the microfibres even more than excess water does.

• For general cleaning use very slightly dampened, spritzed with a spray bottle. If you find you've used too much water, for cleaning a window, say, you'll have to add extra minutes by wiping off the excess drips and smears with a kitchen towel to achieve a sparkling, smear-free result.

• Do use dry as a duster (shake out first if cleaning mirror or glass).

• When you're cleaning floors or other very dirty areas, the cloth (or E-cloth Mop) will trap a lot of dirt and hair. Rinse in a bucket of water between wipes and wring out to eliminate the bulk of the water before wiping again. Pour used dirty water down the toilet rather than the sink which could block.

Where to buy

There are microfibre cloths and microfibre cloths. Many have a denier of approximately 1.00 over a normal cleaning cloth's 200.00 denier. But the denier of an E-cloth is 0.26. It's this high density of fibres which gives them their superior cleaning power and toughness. Most microfibre cloths are made using a moulding technology. E-cloths are woven using high quality cotton. One £5.00 ($8.00) cloth can be washed back to full clean strength about 300 times and lasts for years. Look for the ® trademark in the shops or buy from the website (http://www.e-cloth.com/). Am I jeopardising my journalistic impartiality here backing this one product? Well: no. I'm proud to be a fan and love the comments I receive from readers who have discovered them through my website, column pieces or books. In my opinion they're a no brainer. Simply the healthiest, most efficient and most economical way of cleaning your home.

How many?

On the website you'll see that E-cloth makes a huge variety of cloths tailored for different jobs. There are kitchen cloths, bathroom cloths, window cloths, screen and lens cloths, hob & oven cloths, car and boat cloths, outdoor cloths, tea and hand towel cloths. Now they've even brought out a range of exfoliating and make-up removing cloths. Though each has been formulated for its specific purpose, don't be put off by thinking you need a whole range. Most cleans, apart from delicate lenses and computer screens, can be done with the one basic £5.00/$8.00 cloth. I started out with one cloth and for a long time only had two: one for floors and one for surfaces. I had to carry them from room to room and wash them more, but it's simply a matter of laundering or boiling them up. I use a very small amount of detergent in a saucepan of water and leave them to simmer for 20 minutes or so. This boiling rags part of it is a strangely satisfying thing to do. You can launder E-cloths in the washing machine at 60 degree C (140F), preferably in a washing bag, but for a full clean they need to be boiled at 90 degrees C (194F). Don't use fabric conditioner or bleach. My recommended starter kit, if you can afford it, would include, in addition to a basic cloth, the Deep Clean Mop (my favourite product, swipes across floors in seconds – done), a Window and Glass Cloth and a T-Towel.

Hygiene

The most frequent question I get asked about E-cloths is to do with washing: if dirt and bacteria are trapped in the fibres, surely they'll still be in the cloth. So the next time you go to use it, won't some of the dirt be spread all over your surfaces again? Shouldn't they be laundered at 60 degrees C (140F) after every use, which is impractical?

I asked the E-cloth people about this. Whilst rinsing won't remove all the dirt particles trapped by the cloth, tests have shown that when an E-cloth is re-used, any dirt it has picked up will remain trapped deep within the fibres and will not go back onto your surfaces. So the answer is no, you don't need to launder your E-cloth after every use. Rinsing out in hot water after every use and laundering once a week is sufficient. I throw mine in the sink until my next cup of tea, then chuck over the remains of water boiled in the kettle.

The other reaction is disbelief that cleaning with just water can be as hygienic as using chemical cleaners and anti-bacterials. Well, the manufacturers recently had their cloths tested by Sillliker, the leading international food safety research labs. Results showed that cleaning with an E-cloth and water removes up to 99.9998% of E coli, 99.97% of Listeria and 99.3% of Aspergillus, proving that water, elbow grease and a cloth can be as good as leading cleaning products against microbiological contamination. I, and many other converts, would say 'as good as' isn't the half of it – their performance is superior to chemical products and the air in your home is fresher and healthier to boot.

How to have one of those 'I've got a cleaner' homes

Thanks to the FlyLady (see below) I've got into a habit of going around my flat every day, wiping every surface that's clear. For 6 days out of every 7 I never spend more than ten minutes on cleaning. It took a while to make it a habit, but this means we now have one of those 'I've got a cleaner' homes that never looks or feels dirty, with chemical-free, fresh clear air. Another great thing about E-cloths is that, once you've dampened them, you only need to do a quick wipe-over using one hand. One of my favourite multitaskers is to grab an E-cloth whilst chatting on the phone, especially long gossips with friends, and wander around wiping door-knobs, shower screens, taps, skirting boards etc.

Once a week I mop the wooden and tiled floors and vacuum the carpets. If I'm feeling flush I'll buy some scented flowers and treat the big pine table and any clutter-free wooden surfaces to a beeswax cream polish. I invest a fraction of the money I'm saving on cleaning products in a really luxurious cream polish that feeds and protects the wood.

One of the very best is Roullier White's *Mrs White's The Bees Knees*, a multi-purpose 100% British beeswax polish that's nourishing, eco-friendly, non-abrasive and free from petrochemicals and synthetics (www.roullierwhite.com). The beautiful, subtle, lingering smell of natural beeswax mingles with the scent of the flowers and lasts for days.

If you have a large home and/or a big family it's obviously going to take you longer than it takes me to whizz around my small London flat. But if you can get into the habit of wiping down just the main living areas and bathroom/s every day, leaving the whole home for a quick once-around wipe-down once a week, you will notice a big difference.

For a helping hand with some guerrilla habit-forming tips, check out the remarkable Stateside Domestic Goddess, Marla Cilley, aka FlyLady – your free online coach who'll help you gain control of the clutter (http://www.flylady.net). Her 31-step 'Beginner Baby Steps' system (see the panel at the left of her website) guides you through small tasks that build and turn into routines so slowly that you barely notice.

I only made it as far as Step 8 but I still keep my sink shiny and put my next day's clothes out the night before (mostly). My subsequent E-cloth habit is, I'm sure, partly down to FlyLady's system sticking in the back of my mind. It certainly works for a lot of people. Her free e-mail group full of handy tips and routines is a phenomenon with hundreds and thousands of subscribers.

CHAPTER THREE

What About The Vinegar?

Vinegar has been around for over 10,000 years. It's a natural mild bleach and water softener that dissolves dirt and grease. I may not use it for cleaning, but, along with lemon juice, bicarbonate of soda and the other old favourites, I put it to good use:

• Add half a cup to washing machine fabric conditioner tray as water softener.

• Place a mug of vinegar in the bottom of dishwasher and run on a short, glass-cleaning cycle to clean and deodorise.

• Use as a poultice on stained sinks, soak a cloth and leave covering overnight.

• To remove limescale at base of taps soak a kitchen towel in vinegar and wrap it around the base, leave overnight and wipe the limescale easily away with a damp cloth.

• To remove limescale from tap spouts and showerheads, pour into a plastic bag and secure with an elastic band. Leave overnight, brush off limescale with old nailbrush before polishing up with an e-cloth, a lemon, bicarbonate of soda or Barkeepers Friend.

For more uses, tips, recipes and everything you need to know about vinegar go to The Vinegar Institute:

http:// www.versatilevinegar.org

Where to buy: from supermarkets. If storage space isn't a problem, look out for 5 litre containers of white vinegar in Indian shops and in the warehouse-type discount supermarkets.

Bicarbonate of soda (baking powder) *! Warning – can permanently bleach, use with care on coloured fabrics, carpets and surfaces. Always do a colour-test first.*

This is what I use it for:

• To remove smells from the microwave, dissolve 1 tablespoon of bicarbonate of soda in a cup of water, and cook on high for 3 minutes.

• To clean ovens, sprinkle over surfaces and spritz with a water bottle to dampen. Leave for 10 to 30 minutes before wiping off, longer for burnt-in stains.

• Sprinkle over inside of the fridge and wipe off with damp cloth to clean and deodorise.

• Keep a bowl in the fridge to absorb smells.

• I know it's there as a standby to extinguish grease fires.

Where to buy: You can find small tubs of baking powder in baking section of the supermarket. For cleaning purposes buy bicarbonate of soda in bulk from Amazon.

Carbonated Water (Known in UK as Soda Water, in US & Canada as Seltzer)

Many stains, even red wine stains, can be completely removed with water if they're treated quickly enough. With carbonated water you get an extra boost as the carbonated bubbles sink into the stain and lift the dirt with them as they rise. Keep a bottle in the cupboard for emergencies.

• If you spill something on the carpet, saturate the stain with soda water and cover with kitchen towels, pushing down on the stain. Keep on replacing them with dry ones as they absorb the water.

• If you have a baby or toddler, keep a bottle of soda water next to the high chair to wipe up food spills on bibs and clothing.

Washing-up liquid (In US & Canada Known as Dishwasher Detergent)

One of the best stain removers of all. Use sparingly or it'll need lots of rinsing.

• Apply with cold water to protein stains and hot water to greasy stains (see chapter 12 to learn how to identify).

• Most of us use too much washing-up liquid. In most cases a dribble rather than a squirt is all you need. Make yours go twice as far by diluting 50/50 with water.

Oxygen Bleach *! Colour test before using a higher concentration than the manufacturer's recommendation.*

• A great laundry booster and safe to use on colours at recommended dilution.

• Having said that, mixed with a little water it makes a powerful stain-removing paste. At this strength you must always do a colour test first or permanent damage can result. I use the paste mainly on shadows of stains left on whites.

• Remove difficult stains from carpets and upholstery but always colour test first. If you have a dark mark on a light carpet that's been completely impossible to remove in any other way (and assuming you are not covered by accidental damage in your insurance policy), use the bleach to lighten it into a less-noticeable mark.

• Whiten plastic surfaces that have yellowed. Apply to stain and leave for 30 minutes, rinse. Don't let it come into contact with wood, lacquered/varnished/silk surfaces or mild steel.

• Is a brilliant non-toxic cleaner for outdoor wooden decking areas. When bought in bulk it goes under its chemical name, sodium percarbonate.

Where to buy: Wizz Oxi Ultra Plus from supermarkets. Order pure sodium percarbonate online at http://www.mistralie.co.uk.

Soda Crystals

A coarser, tougher, and cheaper relative of bicarbonate of soda, Soda Crystals soften the water and dissolve grease. They're very cheap and widely available in the UK. To purchase in the US and Canada, go to http://www.msodistributing.com.

• Add a scoop to your washing machine detergent tray. The crystals soften the water and your fabrics and you'll only need to use half the amount of detergent. They also help keep the pipes in your washing machine clear and free of gunge and help remove grease, blood, ink tea and coffee stains.

• Soak old towels and fabrics for half an hour to give them back their softness. Rinse well.

• Clean greasy extractor fans and remove burnt-on food from saucepans, grills and casseroles. Rinse well.

• Pour half a pack down the sink followed by hot water to keep your drains fresh and free of grease.

• Dissolves stains from the inside of cups and teapots. Leave to soak for an hour or so, scrub with a scourer and watch the stains effortlessly peel away. Rinse.

• Remove moss and algae from patios.

3% hydrogen peroxide solution *! Highly inflammable. Highly corrosive to metal, keep away from taps and bathroom fittings.*

This strangely versatile substance is used, amongst other things, as a mouthwash and to make bombs. It's actually a very close relative to water, being just one oxygen atom away. Chemically, this makes it a much less toxic cleaning product than chlorine bleach but, because of its explosive nature, handle with extreme care and follow all safety and storage instructions. It's for this reason you won't see it on the pharmacy shelves but have to ask for it.

• An excellent blood stain remover. Apply to the stain and watch it disappear. Launder the fabric after you've applied the solution or you might get bleach stains. If the blood is on a mattress, apply solution, sprinkle with salt, leave to sit for a minute and watch the stain fizz into the salt, then wash with soap and cold water. Rinse.

• Contact lens solution contains 3% hydrogen peroxide, squeeze directly onto stain to lift blood, red wine and protein stains.

For the many uses of hydrogen peroxide solution see http://www.truthorfiction.com.

Where to buy: From the pharmacy.

Lemon juice

Lemon juice is a natural, mild bleach. Always colour test first as it can lighten fabrics, carpets and some surfaces irreversibly.

• Great for cleaning chopping boards.

• Clean taps and stainless steel to a shine.

• Will sometimes remove fruit and red wine stains on kitchen surfaces. Make a paste with a little flour and, after testing non-white surfaces, leave as poultice covering the stain overnight.

• If fabric isn't affected by lemon juice stain, squeeze onto fruit and wine stains and leave in the sun to dry.

• For badly-stained toilet bowls, mix to a paste with Borax Substitute, and leave overnight.

• Can remove some stains from some types of marble.

• To remove rust, mix with salt to make a poultice. Leave for 30 minutes to 1 hour.

Milk *! Rinse off fabric in cold water afterwards or you'll be left with a milk stain.*
The active enzymes in milk that turn it into cheese make it an excellent stain remover.

• Removes ink, wine, mould, pomegranate and red juice stains. Sour milk by adding a little vinegar and soak stain for 30 minutes. Always rinse thoroughly in COLD water or you'll be left with a smelly milk stain.

• If water and biological detergent foam don't shift

carpet stains, try milk.

• Remove ink stains from tables and other surfaces by soaking a kitchen towel in soured milk, place over stain, weigh down with a vase or bowl, leave for 30 minutes. Rub. Repeat, if necessary several times. Toothpaste speeds up the rubbing process but can lighten some woods and damage veneer, test on hidden part of surface first.

Methylated spirits *! Always colour test before using.*
Commonly known as Denatured Alcohol, Ethanol (Ethyl Alcohol) is mixed with a small amount of Methanol to make it unfit for consumption and then dyed purple or blue.

• Use neat to remove some dye and pigment stains.

• If the stain isn't on silk or wool, mix with ammonia to make an even stronger solution.

Where to buy: Hardware stores.

Shaving cream *! Use the smallest of squirts or you'll never rinse it out.*

• Handy emergency carpet and upholstery stain remover, especially if travelling.

Borax *! Borax is an eye irritant. Wear rubber gloves and keep your hands away from your face.*
Borax, also known as sodium borate, is a natural, alkaline salt that comes from the evaporation of saline lakes.

• Excellent everyday toilet bowl and drain cleaner.

• Good for cleaning badly stained tiles, sinks, floors, walls, windows, mirrors and painted surfaces.

• To remove difficult stains from tiles and carpets, mix three parts borax to one part cold water and work in well. Leave to dry, then vacuum off.

Where to buy: Difficult to find in the shops but easy to source online, see Amazon. It's now known as Borax Substitute in Europe. The properties are identical but Substitute isn't suitable for pest control.

Glycerine (also known as Glycerin/Glycerol)

Sold in pharmacies as a soother for sore throats and coughs, Glycerine is an excellent tannin stain remover.

• Dab difficult old red wine, coffee and tea stains with Glycerine. If you see the stain fading, repeat and repeat again until it's gone.

• For a general stain remover to keep in your cupboard, mix equal parts Glycerine and washing-up liquid (dishwasher detergent) to four parts water.

Where to buy: From the pharmacy.

Ammonia *! Apart from with methylated spirits, never, ever mix ammonia and don't use on wool or silk.*

Ammonia is a natural gas that is reproduced chemically, diluted in water and sold in liquid form. It's an alkaline, which means it's at the opposite end of the scale to acidics (like vinegar and lemon juice) and can therefore neutralise acidic stains.

Household ammonia is 5-10% ammonia; skin contact can cause burns; high concentrations can cause chemical pneumonia; mixing with alkalis releases ammonia gas; mixing with chlorine bleach forms poison gas. Though scientists say household ammonia (5% solution) is about as toxic as vinegar (3% acetic acid), I don't like recommending ammonia for general use. It is good, though, for getting rid of persistent, lingering smells that refuse to budge. Leave a few bowls of ammonia in the room overnight and close the door. Ventilate the room thoroughly afterwards before allowing anybody in there, especially children and animals. Don't use to remove animal smells if the animal is resident as it can make the area more attractive to them.

Where to buy: From hardware stores.

The commercial stain removing and cleaning products I find really useful:

Magic Sponge *! Wear rubber gloves or the grease will get all over your hands. Don't use on varnished, polished or dark surfaces.*

• Magic sponges make excellent oven cleaners, they're chemical-free, fast and very effective. They work on the microfibre principle. There was an email scare in the US a few years ago with a warning that these sponges contain formaldehyde. They don't. Snip off as much sponge as you need (they're not reusable like the e-cloth) and simply dampen and wipe.

• Remove burnt-on food from cookware.

• Remove rubber and skid marks from wood and vinyl floors.

• Removes a variety of stains from walls, wood, vinyl floors.

Where to buy: Poundland (£1.00/$1.61) http://lakeland.co.uk (£4.49/$7.29)

Goo Gone

A safe, citrus-based sticky stuff remover that many Americans swear by. It's difficult to find in the shops outside the US but you can get it on eBay. Apply to the stains and leave to penetrate but don't let it dry out.

• Removes, amongst other things, gum, blood, ink, crayon, make-up and shoe polish from all sorts of surfaces.

• Some vets use it to get tar off pets and wild birds.

Where to buy: http://www.axminster.co.uk (around £7.20/$11.68)

Graffiti Go!

A solvent-free, pH neutral, non toxic solution that cleans off with water.

• Removes tough stains like marker pen, paint, leather dye, crayon and chewing gum.

Where to buy: http://www.decoratingdirect.co.uk (around £9.37/$15.20)

Astonish Paste

A versatile non-toxic, cleaning paste.

• Great for really dirty enamel baths, sinks, ovens and tiles, plastic garden furniture, window surrounds.

Where to buy: Lakeland & larger supermarkets

Barkeepers Friend

Safe to use around food areas, good for cleaning inside the fridge.

• Cleans stainless steel, porcelain, ceramic tiles, plastic, copper, china, fiberglass, imitation marble, tile, grout, chrome, and composition sinks.

• Mix with water into a paste to remove stubborn stains.

Where to buy: Around £3.00 from hardware stores and supermarkets.

Quickleen-S

A non-toxic cleaner only available online. I use this as a last resort on all sorts of surfaces – stainless steel, copper, brass, silver, aluminium, ceramic tiles, carpets and more.

• If you have an impossible stain that nothing else has shifted this is worth trying. It has even removed hair dye stains from my painted wooden surfaces. I use it to spring clean my (non-varnished) pine table. It removes wine rings, water rings, ink and food stains. The wood does dry out and needs replenishing afterwards with a restoring deep polish. If used on surfaces not specifically recommended by the manufacturer, ALWAYS test on a hidden area first.

Where to buy: Online only, £17.01/$27.60. THIS IS MY MOST POWERFUL SECRET INGREDIENT! One tub lasts a long time: http://Quickleen.co.uk.

Wine Away

A non-toxic product that removes red wine and other red stains from carpets and fabrics. Made from fruit and vegetable extracts with no bleach or phosphates, this is an excellent spray-on red stain remover that works on old stains as well.

Where to buy:
£10.99/$17.79 http://www.lakeland.co.uk

Ecover Biological (with Enzymes) and Non-Biological (without Enzymes)

The UK's leading brand of green cleaners. (In the US, one of the most popular brands is http://www.seventhgeneration.com.) Completely biodegradable washing detergent which causes minimum impact on aquatic life, is not tested on animals and suitable for septic tanks. Biological is recommended for whites and colourfast laundry. The enzymes help break stains down. Non-biological is recommended for coloureds and hand washing. For whites and colourfast laundry add a scoop of Oxygen bleach. Unlike most detergents, Ecover doesn't contain optical brighteners (see Chapter 9). Add Soda Crystals to your wash and use less detergent. This will more than deflect the higher cost of this excellent brand.

Ariel Biological Liquid Detergent

I keep a bottle of this as a bad stain pre-soaker and stain remover. If any stains remain after soaking, I put a little liquid directly onto the stain before laundering. For carpet stains that won't come out with Soda Water, whoosh up some Ariel with lukewarm water and apply the froth to the stain. Rinse.

Last but not least:

The only household product in the world with its own fan club (http://www.WD40.com):

WD-40

! Makes surfaces dangerously slippery. Follow up with a grease-cutting washing-up liquid solution and good rinse.

Developed in the 1950s as a rust preventative for the aircraft industry, WD-40 gets its name from the inventor's 40 attempts at water displacement before he reached the magic (secret) formula. Its primary purpose is to clean, protect and loosen rusted parts, free sticky mechanisms and stop squeaks. But it also:

• Removes Blu Tack and other sticky deposits.

• Removes crayon marks from hard surfaces, inc wallpaper.

• Removes candle soot.

• Cleans scuff marks from floors.

• Cleans dog mess from shoes.

For more, see http://www.wd40.com/uses-tips

CHAPTER FOUR

Toxic Chemicals in the Home

All major supermarkets now sell own-brand green cleaning products. Ecover is widely available as is Seventh Generation in the US. Significantly in Europe, new legislation came into force in 2007, regulated by a European Community directive called REACH. REACH stands for Registration, Evaluation, Authorisation and Restriction of Chemical substances. Its mission statement is 'to improve the protection of human health and the environment through the better and earlier identification of the intrinsic properties of chemical substances.'

An announcement from REACH stated that *"Six substances of very high concern will be banned* [from 2011] *unless an authorisation has been granted to individual companies for their use. These substances are carcinogenic, toxic for reproduction or persist in the environment and accumulate in living organisms."* Better than not at all, and quicker than some. These substances are:

5-ter-butyl-2,4,6-trinito-m-xylene (musk xylene) *A synthetic musk fragrance that mimics natural musk. Largely phased out but still present in some cosmetics and fragrances.*

hexabromocyclododecane (HBCDD) *Primarily used as a flame retardant in polystyrene foam thermal home insulation. Other uses are upholstered furniture, automobile interior textiles, car cushions and insulation blocks in trucks, packaging material, video cassette recorder housing and electric and electronic equipment.*

bis(2-ethylexyl) phthalate (DEHP) *widely used as a plasticizer in manufacturing of articles made of PVC. Accounts for appx 18% of all plasticiser usage in W Europe. Used in many medical devices – catheters, dialysis bags and tubing, blood bags, transfusion tubing, air tubes.*

benzyl butyl phthalate (BBP) BBzP *was commonly used as a plasticizer for vinyl foams often used as floor tiles. Also found in traffic cones, food conveyer belts and artificial leather. Its use has declined rapidly in the last decade. There are only two producers remaining in the EU.*

4,4'-diaminodiphenylmethane (MDA) *a curing agent used in some epoxy-resins.*

dibutyl phthalate (DBP) *a commonly used plasticizer. Also used as an additive to adhesives or printing inks. It is soluble and found in solvents. Also used in an antiparasitic drug called ectoparasiticide.*

REACH calls the worrying chemicals SVHC – Substances of Very High Concern. You can see the full list on Wikipedia:

http://en.wikipedia.org/wiki/Substance_of_very_high_concern

As I update this book in 2020, the widespread use of toxic, banned flame retardants has been in the news again, particularly in relation to the Grenfell fire tragedy. This Guardian article by George Monbiot 'Toxic Sofas are a Secret Scandal' is a must-read https://www.theguardian.com/commentisfree/2020/feb/26/toxic-sofa-eu-red-tape-flame-retardants? Be sure to look at the Comments section as well.

Replace what you can replace and be aware

A problem beyond individual chemical poisons is the cumulative (or 'cocktail') effect of exposure to multiple chemicals. This relates to phthalates in particular. Phthalates are used in the manufacture of plastics to increase their flexibility. As well as plastic containers they're found in all sorts of things – disinfectants, aerosols, moth repellants, air fresheners, cosmetics, paints and lacquers.

It's impossible to know what's in what. The best course of action beyond replacing what products you can with healthy, environmentally friendly alternatives is to Be Aware. If you have the need to use any powerful chemical household products or solvents, take precautions, open windows and **don't** inhale.

Navigating The REACH Labyrinth

A task way beyond this book – but there is plenty of information and opportunity to get involved online:

The Health and Environment Alliance http://www.env-health.org/), otherwise known as HEAL, is a network of NGOs (non-governmental organisations) and other not-for-profit organisations in the field of environment and health. In collaboration with other partner organisations across Europe, HEAL has set up The Chemicals Health Monitor Project (http://www.chemicalshealthmonitor.org/):

"The project contributes to the tools and structures

necessary so that important health stakeholders can understand the REACH labyrinth and have their views about key decisions voiced. The project will also provide authoritative information (in a form accessible to the nonspecialist public) to support measures to reduce harmful effects of hazardous chemicals on human health and the environment, and to choose safer alternatives."

They have produced a very useful free PDF downloadable book called **Navigating Reach – An Activist's Guide to Using and Improving The New EU Chemicals Legislation** The introduction summarises the good news:

"The improvement of Health and Safety information; safer substitutes for the most dangerous chemicals; industry, consumer and retailer right to know about the hazardous chemicals present in products."

But also the loopholes and flaws:

"Companies may be allowed to continue importing, producing and using many hazardous substances associated with cancer, birth defects, reproductive illnesses and hormonal imbalances, even when safer alternatives exist.

Registration will only apply to 30,000 out of over 100,000 chemicals known to be on the market today and only rudimentary information may be required for 60% of those 30,000. Although the authorities could request more, information is likely to be insufficient to make a decision.

The decision on whether to make manufacturers replace chemicals that can mimic hormones (endocrine disruptors) with safer alternatives, whenever they exist, has been postponed to a future date."

CHEM Trust (http://www.chemtrust.org.uk) is the charity which now runs the campaigns against toxic chemicals started by the World Wildlife Fund.

"CHEM Trust is uniquely placed in the UK to address the chemicals and health issue and will fill an important niche vacated by WWF, Greenpeace (UK), and Friends of the Earth (England and Wales). We will build on their work and continue to make a real difference to human health, wildlife and the wider environment."

It has this to say about the REACH agreement:

"The final text of the new REACH law brought good news and bad news for the environment, wildlife and human health. The good news is that chemicals which build up in living organisms and those which linger in the environment for a long time will have to be replaced whenever safer alternatives are available. The bad news is that chemicals which may cause cancer or birth defects, affect DNA, disturb the hormone system or cause other serious illnesses (so-called CMRs and hormone disrupting chemicals) will continue to be allowed on the market even if safer alternatives are available."

The International Chemical Secretariat (www.chemsec.org/) has produced a Sin List of the 378 Substances of Very High Concern (http://www.sinlist.org/)

"The SIN (Substitute It Now!) List is an NGO driven project to speed up the transition to a toxic free world. The List 2.0 consists of 378 chemicals that are identified as Substances of Very High Concern based

on the criteria established by the EU chemical regulation, REACH. The SIN List is an important tool for speeding up the REACH legislative process, and is based on a straightforward concept: substitute hazardous chemicals with safer alternatives. Think of it as a fast track to a toxic-free world.

Substitute It Now! *The 378 chemicals on the SIN List 2.0 are currently being used in everything from detergents and paints to computers and toys. Sometimes in high levels. Yet consumers have no knowledge of this. The SIN List puts pressure on legislators to move forward with speed and urgency. It provides progressive retail companies with a helpful list of hazardous chemicals to avoid as they aim for a sustainable future. It also challenges certain chemical companies to shape up."*

The REACH website is at the European Commission for the Environment

http://ec.europa.eu/environment/chemicals/reach/reach_intro.htm

Beyond Europe

In the US, progress on the vital matter of chemicals in the air that we breathe is even slower. Professor Anne C Steinemann of the University of Washington's Department of Civil and Environmental Engineering and the Evans School of Public Affairs, specialises in environmental pollutants and public health. In 2008, she carried out three sets of studies on air fresheners and fragranced cleaning products. Her findings were widely reported at the time. In a letter to a state Board of Education she said: *"I am very concerned that air fresheners and cleaning products with an added fragrance are being considered for use in your schools. Air fresheners and fragranced cleaning products, even ones certified as 'green,' emit numerous toxic chemicals — including carcinogenic Hazardous Air Pollutants that, according to the Environmental Protection Agency, have no exposure level considered 'safe'.*

"To understand this striking gap between chemicals emitted and chemicals disclosed, I investigated the US regulations pertaining to air fresheners and fragranced cleaning products. I discovered that companies are not required to test for toxic chemicals in air fresheners or fragranced cleaners, nor are they required to disclose any of the ingredients—not even chemicals that are classified as toxic or hazardous. In other words, you will not find hazardous chemicals listed on the product labels or material safety data sheets, and that is legal, because they do not need to be disclosed. The company providing you with air fresheners and cleaners is probably asserting that they are "safe." But that term has no legal definition when it concerns air fresheners and fragranced cleaning products.

"My chemical analyses of a range of air fresheners (including sprays, solid disks, plug-ins, and oils) and fragranced cleaning products (including all-purpose cleaners, glass cleaners, floor cleaners, bathroom cleaners, detergents, and disinfectants) found that each one emitted chemicals that are carcinogens, neurotoxins, and respiratory toxins. Even air fresheners and fragranced cleaning products marketed as 'organic,' 'green,' 'all-natural,' or with 'essential oils' were just as toxic, and in some cases more toxic

than the regular varieties. More than 100 volatile organic compounds were emitted by air fresheners and fragranced cleaning products, but none of these chemicals were listed on any product label or material safety data sheet."

Anne and her team have found that many fragranced household and personal care products, including those labelled 'Green' have at least one chemical classified as a probable carcinogen.

Read more:

http://donedust.blogspot.com/2010/11/chemical-sleuthing-reveals-toxins-in.html

The *Safer Chemicals Healthy Families* coalition represents more than 11 million individual Americans. Their website (http://www.saferchemicals.org/) has all the latest information on chemicals in the home and details on how you can take part in their powerful and active campaign for urgent reform of the Toxic Substances Control Act (TSCA). The US Environmental Protection Agency's Introduction to Indoor Air Quality (http://www.epa.gov/iaq/ia-intro.html) says that concentrations of indoor VOCs are consistently up to ten times higher indoors than outdoors. VOC stands for Volatile Organic Compounds, 'some of which', the Agency states, 'may have short and long term adverse health effects'.

Another problem is the growth of Greenwashing. The environmentally aware consumer who's willing to pay a bit more for 'natural' products is a new, powerful category in the market researcher's row of tick boxes. Now some companies are spending more time and money spinning green advertising and packaging than on environmentally sound practices. Greenwashing is nothing new. The phrase was coined back in the 1980s when an environmentalist realised that the green cards in the bathrooms of a New York hotel asking guests to consider re-using their towels proved to be more about profit than the environment. What is new is that consumers in the know can fight back. In the US, the trusted site Good Guide (www.goodguide.com) have come up with a free barcode App. You scan your iPhone camera over the barcode to get instant and up to date information on the manufacturer's policy on health, environment and social responsibility. There are scores out of ten plus a list of ingredients to avoid in each category. In household cleaners, for example, there's Ammonia, Benzene, Potassium Hydroxide, Quaternary Ammonium Chloride, Sodium Hydroxide, Sodium Hypochlorite, Terpenes and Triclosan.

The International Association for Soaps, Detergents and Maintenance Products, is the official representative of the industry in Europe (http://www.aise.eu). Their Air Fresheners Product Stewardship Programme states that it builds on *'a series of voluntary initiatives already undertaken by AISE in the domain of safety assessment and sustainability allowing consumers to make the best-informed choices about safe product usage.'*

CHAPTER FIVE

How to Make Healthy, Home-made Air Fresheners

I haven't bought air fresheners for many years but do like to fragrance rooms sometimes, especially if I've been cooking kippers or have burnt the toast. I keep a jar of home-made air freshener which I boil up in a saucepan and waft around the flat. The bad smells are replaced with a lovely, subtle lingering scent which you just catch for a day or so afterwards when you come in from outside.

Into a small saucepan of water add:

Two limes, quartered, juices squeezed (or use bottled lime juice)

15 drops of patchouli essential oil

A teaspoon of cinnamon powder or 10 drops of cinnamon essential oil

A teaspoon of grated ginger

5 Cloves

A teaspoon of vanilla essence

Bring to boil and simmer for 10 minutes. Turn the heat off, add 2 teaspoons of bicarbonate of soda & carry through home, wafting it about, priest-like, as you go.

It's a rich, sophisticated smell. When the mixture has cooled I pour it into a jar for use next time, topping up here and there as I fancy. It keeps for 6 to 12 weeks. Much longer than this and mould will set in. Adapt as you wish, substituting lemons for limes, leaving bits out altogether it you've run out etc.

To make your own personal air freshener, think about the smells you love. For inspiration, have a look on your bathroom shelves. My recipe started with my favourite face cleanser, Antipodes Organic Hallelujah Lime and Patchouli.

(http://www.beautybazaar.co.uk)

I'm still experimenting. One of my favourite smells is Hoof Oil, a thick, creosote-type smell, not all that distant from Inside Summer Shed, another of my favourites that never fails to stir up memories of distant, childhood summers. I'm still looking for the right combination of ingredients to replicate the smell of the Paris flat I lived in for a while in my early 20s. So far I've got coffee, garlic, leather, aniseed. What stops me from even starting to try this one is the difficulty of replicating the subtle, tinny waft of River Seine that flowed beside the street down below. Maybe next time I go to France I'll bottle up a little bit of Seine and start from there.

For a lighter, summer smell you could start with a base of essential citrus oils like lemon, or lavender. In the summer, though, I don't bother. As I'm lucky enough not to suffer from hay fever, the windows tend to be open and fresh air with a top note of cut summer grass is the loveliest, healthiest smell of all.

CHAPTER SIX

The Cheapest Way To Double Your Storage Space

Vacuum bags can double, even triple, your storage space and protect against moths, moisture, odour, dirt, rust and corrosion. They can be used for almost anything that you stuff into cupboards – fabrics, clothes, paperwork, photos, memorabilia, china and silver, books, tents, soft toys, old electronics/computers. The only things to avoid are fur, leather, and anything containing feathers and/or down. The problem is the cost. Good, strong bags with vacuum seals are expensive and the cheaper ones are a bit of a gamble. The sides split more easily and the seals can fail.

Bin liners don't have the special seals, but you can use them in the same way. Your possessions do get some protection and, as long as you place them in situ as soon as you've vacuumed the air out, you can gain all of that precious extra storage space before they start to let the air in and expand out again.

Take a good strength bin liner and place your fabrics, soft toys or whatever inside. Don't go for the very thick type of garden sacks because they're impossible to tie at the ends. If you have any small items or irreplaceable pieces of paper, gather them inside a smaller plastic bag first or they could get sucked away.

Scrunch the top of the bag together around the hose

of your vacuum cleaner and switch it on. Do it in spurts or, if your vacuum cleaner is anything like mine, it'll overheat and stop working until it's cooled down again. When the bag has collapsed to a fraction of its size, tie the ends as tightly as you can. To gain as much space as possible, pile the shrivelled bags on top of each other until there's no space above or below them on the shelf. There is then only so much surrounding air into which they can expand and you can pack so much more in. Keep bags away from sharp objects and don't store near any heat source. Make sure everything is clean and bone dry before storing and don't forget to label the bags or make a little inventory before you forget what's where.

CHAPTER SEVEN

The Humane Way to Get Rid of Rats, Mice and Ants

I live in a very old building and used to have mice everywhere. They'd appear from nowhere and stroll about every room as if they owned it. We tried all sorts of humane traps and then bought nasty poisons and traps which we couldn't bring ourselves to use, even though the mice were getting cheekier and cheekier. The problem was solved by Pest Stop 2000

(http://www.pest-stop.co.uk/electronic-pest-control/33/pest-stop-2000)

and we haven't had a hint of a mouse for years. It's a small plastic device that, when plugged in, emits fluctuating, ultrasonic and electromagnetic waves that mice can't bear. One is enough to cover a whole house up to 2,000 sq feet. It can also be used to deter rats, squirrels and crawling insects and has a special mosquito setting. It's safe if you have dogs, cats, fish and birds, but not small rodents like hamsters. Pest Stop make products to deter all sorts of creatures from badgers to woodlice, there's even an Ultrasonic Flea Repeller collar for cats and dogs.

There are versions for sale in most countries. We paid about £40.00 ($64.00) for ours. Make sure it's the electromagnetic type that transmits a signal along every electrical cable in the building. We did try a cheaper

£10.00 ($16.00) ultrasonic plug-in deterrent which didn't work at all.

If you find ants in your home there are two obvious first steps:

• follow the trail to its end and remove the jar of soy sauce, pot of jam or whatever sweet and sticky food source is attracting them.

• go outside, find out where they're coming in and block it with filling cement.

The sight of ants in the kitchen is always the first sign to me that summer's truly arrived. As we live in a flat, I don't have access to all of our outside areas. I've tried every kind of natural repellant: garlic, cinnamon, vinegar, mint, baby powder, drawing a line in chalk across their path. None worked. The best remedy I've come across is a home-made version of what many professional pest busters do. Place a spoonful of borax and syrup or sugar on the trail. The ants will gorge on the syrup and ingest the borax at the same time. Some will be taken back to the Queen and the borax will make her sterile.

CHAPTER EIGHT

A Healthy Kitchen

For several years now I have been cooking for somebody recovering from cancer. The World Cancer Research Fund is a charity dedicated to stopping cancer before it starts. Its latest report, '*Food, Nutrition, Physical Activity and The Prevention of Cancer, A Global Perspective*', is totally conclusive that a healthy diet and exercise routine helps prevent cancer and contributes to a successful recovery. The chances of other serious illnesses like heart disease, diabetes and strokes, developing and progressing are also reduced. The report is free to download

(http://www.wcrf-uk.org/cancer_prevention/index.php)

and the website has lots of recipes and free advice. The Healthy New You Plan leads you through a gradual 12 week programme with tips, quizzes and weekly target sheets.

In my role as a carer, I went on a specialist cancer and chemo-related nutrition course. The very first thing we were told was that, as a complete lifestyle change would be difficult to sustain and therefore quite possibly more stressful than it's worth, we should absorb all that we were taught and then make small, manageable shifts that we could comfortably deal with in our lives. Here are the small but significant changes I have made at home:

• I have reduced our intake of sugar, by no means completely but by switching small, regular habits (http://breastcancer.about.com/od/cancerfightingfoods/a/cancer_sugar_myth.htm)

• I've replaced Maple Syrup on porridge with Agave Nectar. It's delicious and actually sweeter than sugar but is 100% natural plant extract, costs less and is available in all the main supermarkets. Agave does have its detractors, cheaper products labelled Agave could be chemical fructose. Read the label and only buy certified organic.

• Artificial Sweeteners like Aspartame are another area of controversy. I prefer to avoid them wherever possible.

• I always thought reusing old mini water bottles was a no-brainer, saving both my cash and the environment. On my nutrition course we were strongly advised not to do this, and not to drink from them if they've been left in the sun.

It's confusing because several chemicals associated with plastics have raised concerns: DEHA, DEHP and BPA. If you look at Cancer Research UK's website page, Cancer Myths:

(https://www.cancerresearchuk.org/about-cancer/causes-of-cancer/cancer-myths)
you'll read that the whole plastic bottle scare began with a scientist on a Japanese TV programme in 2002 voicing concerns about the safety of freezing water in plastic bottles. The dangers of plastic leaching into the food and water then spread rapidly on the internet.

Disposable drinking water bottles don't contain the dodgy BPA (see below). Tests done in the US on bottles made of FED-approved polyethylene terephthalate (PET) found traces of potentially hazardous substances but they were miniscule and well within regulation safety limits. Many health professionals say the greatest risk in reusing plastic bottles comes from from germs. "The types of plastic bottles in which drinking water is typically sold are safe to reuse as long as their condition hasn't deteriorated and you can clean them,' says CancerResearch UK. 'They should be cleaned with hot, soapy water and thoroughly dried every time you refill them, to prevent bacteria from growing.'

These days of course, we should be carrying our own non-plastic water bottles and reducing our use of plastic whenever possible.

Bis(2-ethylhexyl) adipate (DEHA)

Bis (2-ethylhexyl) adipate (DEHA) was rumoured to leach out of plastic containers heated in the microwave. This triggered the widespread scare that erupted a few years ago about microwaving foods in their plastic containers. The rumours have been traced to their source and the EU has confirmed that it poses no 'general' risk to human health. DEHA has been demonstrated to induce liver adenomas and carcinomas in mice but not in rats. Cancer Research UK says "There is no convincing evidence that DEHA is actually present in plastic bottles or plastic wraps. Even if it was, in the late 1990s, the US Environmental Protection Agency (EPA) removed DEHA from its list of toxic chemicals. It said that DEHA 'cannot reasonably be anticipated to cause cancer' as well as a number of other health problems."

EHP (Di(2-ethylhexyl) phthalate)

Mainly used to soften PVC, this is one of REACH's "six substances of very high concern" and will be banned within the next three to five years unless an authorisation has been granted to individual companies for their use. Each substance in the six substance list has been given a "sunset date" ranging from 2014 to 2015. "From this date the substance may only be placed on the market or used if an authorisation has been granted or an application for authorisation has been made before the latest application date. This is the date by which anyone wishing to keep using a listed chemical after the sunset date must make an application."

DEHP accounts for about 18% of all plasticiser usage in W Europe and whilst it hasn't been used in children's toys for several years (banned in 2007) it's still used in many medical devices.

Bisphenol A (BPA) found in some plastic containers, especially those used for babies and small children, has been more of a worry. After a year-long campaign by Breast Cancer UK, backed by the National Childbirth Trust, CHEM Trust and others, the EU Commission banned BPA from all baby bottles in June 2011. The six major makers of baby bottles and cups in the US no longer use BPA in their products and Canada banned it in 2008.

On BPA in the lining of cans, one of the UK's most trusted major supermarkets has this to say: 'BPA is a material that attracts a good deal of controversy and misinformation. It's important that there is a protective film inside a can to separate the food from the metal and thereby prevent the can corroding and migrating into the food. BPA is not itself used to coat the inside of cans but is one of the building blocks used to make resins which are then further reacted to form an inert and resistant protective film. Only minute traces of unreacted BPA are in the finished polymer. We do continue to closely monitor this chemical as new evidence comes to light.'

To give you an idea of 'minute', a major US soup company tested its containers for BPA and found 40 to 60 parts per trillion (equivalent of 40 – 60 seconds in 32,000 years).

• I cook with olive oil or coconut oil now and make sure it's never heated to a high, smoking temperature. This is because of the toxic chemical by-product of heating oils. Dien Aldehydes occur when any kind of oil is heated but in varying degrees. Coconut oil is best to use (if you can cope with the taste), followed by olive oil.

Reader's Tip: Thanks to Hattie Pond for pointing out that Cold Pressed Grapeseed Oil is excellent for cooking at high temperatures.

• I've reduced our intake of starchy refined carbs – white flour, biscuits, pasta, cakes etc. I've swapped white rice and pasta for brown wholegrain and cook more veg. Two excellent online recipe resources are the World Cancer Research Fund and Riverford Organics

(http://www.wcrf-uk.org/index.php) (http://www.riverford.co.uk).

Both have interactive search facilities where you type in your main ingredient and get a list of healthy recipes. Riverford's are seasonal and constantly updated with links to the current week's home delivery organic fruit and veg boxes. In this way you can vary your diet with little effort, cooking with pesticide-free, uber-fresh, locally (mainly) sourced fruit and veg that's been grown for flavour rather than shelf life. You can swap, change and add to your boxes' ingredients online at any time so you don't feel locked in. Delivery is free and they also claim that overall their boxes work out 19% cheaper than the supermarkets.

• The problem with non-stick coated frying pans is a chemical called PFOA (perfluorocatanoic acid) and its links to thyroid disease.

(http://www.sciencedaily.com/releases/2010/01/100
121082853.htm).

Until I could afford a good replacement I took care not to overheat my pan, because once PFOA gets into the air it stays there, lingering forever. PFOA is all over the place from carpets and fabrics to greaseproof paper. The US Environmental Protection Agency is working towards a complete elimination of PFOA by 2015.

The World Wildlife Fund has called for PFOA to be classified as a substance of very high concern because of its persistent, toxic and bio-accumulative properties. In a DETOX bio-monitoring study, traces were found in the majority of children.

PFOA is in so many things, cosmetics, clothing, cleaners, it's difficult to eliminate all products from your home that contain it completely. See *Chapter 11 – A Healthy Bathroom*, for more guidelines. Before buying major items like carpets and furniture, find out the PFOA content or go for wooden floors and natural materials. For more details see the Environmental Working Group's page PFCs, Global Contaminants:

(http://www.ewg.org/pfc-manufacturers)

I now have a new PFOA-free non-stick pan and I love it. Green Pans are made with heavy gauge, recycled aluminium or stainless steel and finished with a natural ceramic coating called Thermolon. They're heat resistant up to 450 degrees C (842F). Hot enough for heat searing and flambéing with no risk of polluting the air. I do still use a non-stick pan for quick-frying fish like seabass which needs a crunchy skin, as the Green Pan simply won't cut it. I just take extra care not to overheat the pan. For more information on Green Pans see my Done and Dusted blog entry

(http://donedust.blogspot.com/2010/11/green-pans-non-stick-and-pfoa-free.html).

• Though the DEHA plastics in microwaves scare originates from an urban myth, I have cut down generally on microwave use. This isn't because of any new little-publicised danger of microwaving, but since it was pointed out that the food is cooked by its molecules being jiggled around, I just haven't fancied it. (That's why there are always instructions to leave food standing for several minutes after it's been cooked, which I always used to blatantly ignore.)

• Call me overcautious if you will, but another just to be on the safe side adjustment I've made is to swap my plastic kettle for a stainless steel one.

• Many studies on the benefits/non-benefits of organic food often look at nutrition only and don't take pesticides into account at all. However, a recent major study (July 2014) by a team from Newcastle University found statistically significant, meaningful differences, and concluded that organic fruit & veg contain more of the antioxidant compounds linked to better health as well as lower levels of toxic metals and pesticides. Avoiding the chemicals sprayed on fruit and veg and fed to factory farmed animals is the main reason why many choose organic, with nutritional benefits coming in as an extra bonus. Of course individual pesticides are tested for safety before use, but it's the cocktails of chemicals that nobody really knows about.

I generally avoid the non-organic foods with the most pesticides on them. I still buy non-organic fruits and vegetables that have protective skins like avocados, onions, melons, mangoes, peas, aubergine, whole sweetcorn and bananas. Aware that leafy foods are the ones that receive direct hits from the sprayers, I pay the bit extra for organic lettuce and spinach. Organic strawberries are too expensive to bother with but some supermarket brand organic apple juice, for example, is cheaper than many main-brand non-organic. Organic bread costs more but I now make each loaf go further by slicing it and freezing it as soon as I get it home.

For all information on which pesticides are sprayed on which foods and which supermarkets are addressing the issue see Pesticide Action Network UK (Pan-UK) at (http://www.pan-uk.org/food/best-worst-food-for-pesticide-residues).

A list of the 47 American foods with the most pesticides starting from worst (peach) to best (onion) can be found at the Environmental Working Group's Food News US Shoppers Guide to Pesticides (http://www.foodnews.org). Their handy Free App listing all veg and fruits, organic and non-organic, works in both the US and UK but UK readers should note that the results are based on USDA (US Department of Agriculture) tests.

• I've thrown out the salt and replaced it with Himalayan Crystal Salt. I was worried about the cost and the taste of 'healthy pink salt', but the health issue is a powerful one. Himalayan salt crystals were formed from the evaporation of the primal sea over 250 million years ago when pollution didn't exist. It has 81 good minerals in it (with all sorts of health benefits) whilst table salt has 2 bad ones (sodium chloride and iodine).

For some reason, maybe the colour, I thought it would have an odd, herby flavour to it but it doesn't at all. It's as crunchy and salty as any other salt with a refined, delicate subtleness to it.And, at £2.50/$4.05 a jar, affordable.

(http://www.himalayancrystalsalt.co.uk/home.asp)

• We were taught the real importance of eating our greens and the benefits of getting as much chlorophyll and oxygen in our systems as we could. The leafier, greener and fresher the veg the more chlorophyll it contains. Iceberg lettuces, a supermarket favourite because of their long shelf life, score very low here. The recommended 5 fresh fruit and veg a day should actually be more like 12, with a ratio of 80/20 veg/fruit. The best way to get anywhere near this is to drink a green smoothie every day. I went on a course to learn how to make these.

The core ingredients of the green smoothie are: cucumber, celery, sprouting sunflower seeds, pea green sprouts. To which can be added whatever greens and natural flavourings you like. The great news is you don't need a juicer. Blenders retain the pulp which is where much of the goodness is and are so much easier to clean. A good, high end blender breaks everything down into liquid, including whole carrots and apples (with the core and the pips – which are very rich in Vitamin B17). I have to make do with the rickety old blender I've had for over 20 years but it doesn't do too badly. It can cope with melon seeds but can't deal with any part of an apple, let alone its core. The sample made for us had all sorts in it – avocado, spinach, mange tout, spring onions, ginger, lime, garlic, salt, pepper, basil. It tasted good but finding the right recipe to make every morning at home took quite a while and a little compromise. This one has most of the good stuff in, isn't expensive, is quick to make and, most importantly of all, tasty.

For 1 glass: Cucumber (a slice appx the length of a large egg); A stick of organic celery; a banana; a big, round slice of fresh Fair Trade pineapple (or any fresh fruit in season); a handful of sunflower (or other) sprouting seeds. Put a little water in the jug first, add everything else and whizz.

If your smoothie is part of diet routine fighting severe illness, as mine is, think about adding either green tea concentrate or a good quality chlorophyll tablet supplement like Sun Chlorella. These tiny rocket bombs of concentrated green algae are suitable for children, and pets as well, but not for anybody on Warfarin (https://www.sunchlorella.co.uk/).

CHAPTER NINE

Why Optical Brighteners are Optical Illusions – 30 Degree Washing the (nearly) Eco Way

So many of us use too much detergent and heat. The recommended amount of detergent for a lightly soiled load of washing if you live in a soft water area is minescule. If you don't live in a soft water area, add Soda Crystals and you'll still need only a tiny scoop.

Washing at 40C (104F) rather than 60C (140F) saves a massive third of the energy consumed. Laundering at 30 degrees rather than 40 degrees saves each household between £8.00/$12.95 and £18.00/$29.14 a year. Not a huge part of any annual budget but still real money in your pocket for no actual loss whilst helping to reduce the pressure on the national grid. *Which?* says that for every 50 families who make this 10 degree change, their local power station emissions quota will be measurably affected for the good. You won't notice any difference. Your fabrics will look, and will be, just as clean.

The big manufacturers now make special 30 degree, even 15 degree (49F) detergents. Ariel's 15 degree Excell Gel came out as top product in Which?'s 30 degree tests even though it was tested at a full 10 degrees lower temperature than its rivals. Fabrics washed in detergents that contain optical brighteners (which means all the main brands) do, without a doubt, come out looking brighter and whiter. It's a very clever trick. Complex concoctions of chemicals (the exact ingredients are often trade secrets) are soaked up by the fibres but don't get rinsed out. They 're a kind of dye which converts invisible ultraviolet light into the visible spectrum. The fibres then have more light to reflect and so appear brighter. Because this additional light comes from the violet-blue spectrum, which makes the yellow spectrum appear brighter, the fabric will also appear whiter.

Ecover detergents don't contain any chemical optical brighteners or any trade secrets at all. Like the leading US eco brand Seventh Generation, they're based on natural plant and mineral ingredients that are kind to the planet and your skin. Apart from its eco-credentials I love the herbal smell of the washing as I hang it to dry. What I do, though, is keep a bottle of Ariel liquid as an emergency booster and soaker. If I have a nasty-looking stain I'll either leave it to soak in Ariel first and/or apply a little neat liquid directly to both sides of the stain before laundering. Ecover also makes a powerful Stain Remover, which can be applied directly to the stain or used as a soak.

If you want to continue (or start) using an eco-brand it's still possible to get entirely satisfactory results while washing at lower temperatures. If you use Soda Crystals to soften the water, the money you save on the quantity of detergent needed more than makes up for the extra cost. Plus there are other benefits. Here are my tips for 30 degree C (86F) washing the (nearly) eco way:

- Add 25 – 50g (one third of a cup – half a cup)

(depending on the water hardness) of Soda Crystals to the detergent tray along with your washing powder. The natural non-toxic crystals soften the water and your fabrics, help shift grease, blood, ink, tea and coffee stains from cotton and linen and help keep the pipes of your washing machine clear. You can also reduce the amount of detergent needed to the level recommended for soft water. Too much detergent is as bad as, if not worse than, too little detergent. (Have your towels ever come out stiff and scratchy? Too much detergent.) Check the levels. You might find you need less than you realise. Absorbent fabrics like towelling need barely any detergent at all to come out soft and well-rinsed.

• Biological detergents contain enzymes which break down grease and protein stains and so are good to use for dirty, stained laundry. Ecover recommends its non-biological detergent for whites and colourfast laundry. Instead of enzymes it contains a higher dose of integrated bleach activator.

• For an extra, whitening boost to whites and colourfast laundry add a scoop of oxygen bleach powder to the detergent tray.

• For extra softness add half a cup of white vinegar to the rinse cycle.

• Don't forget that the clothes and bedding of asthma sufferers still need to be washed at a higher temperature, 60 degrees (140F) minimum, to eliminate dust mites, bacteria, pollen, mould and pet allergens.

• If washing regularly at low temperatures, don't forget to do a high temperature wash once a month, as recommended by washing machine manufacturers, to keep the pipes free of gunge.

• Powders are less likely to clog pipes than liquids.

• If a stain persists on whites, soak in a mild solution of chlorine bleach and water for 15 minutes. On colours, soak in recommended dosage of oxygen bleach. If that doesn't work, make a paste of oxygen bleach, apply and leave for half an hour or so – but when using a more concentrated amount of bleach, always do a colour test first and rinse thoroughly afterwards.

CHAPTER TEN

A little Bit of Dirt… What's Bad About Chemical Anti-Bacterials

It's common knowledge that taking antibiotics when you don't really need them can be counter-productive. Apart from the good bacteria in the gut being wiped out along with the bad, those left behind react and become more resistant. This is why it's so important to continue taking a course of antibiotics even if you start to feel well again. The bacteria that have survived the first few days of attack are the strongest and they're the ones that will evolve in your body with more resistance if you let them. On a larger scale, the power of antibiotics to cure gradually becomes less effective, as has happened with Penicillin and Erythromycin. Effectively you are disabling your own immune system while the drug takes over. Absolutely vital in emergencies of course, but not a good idea for general, casual use.

When you spray a surface with an anti-bacterial spray, 99.9% of the bacteria will be wiped out as advertised. The toughest 0.1%, however, will be left on your kitchen surface to breed and evolve with more resistance, just like the bacteria in the gut. Apart from the environmental concerns of mass anti-bacterial use, some scientists worry that with more anti-bacterial products than ever being used in the home, new strains of superbug will emerge. The other worry is that, as with antibiotics, the harmless bacteria are wiped out along with the bad. If the healthy resistance that our bodies have naturally built up through exposure to germs is removed, our immune systems will weaken.

Anti-bacterials, you may think, have their place. For treating fresh cuts and wounds and for cleaning hands after handling raw meat, excrement etc. But even this is questionable. A study by the University of Michigan found that washing with soap and water is just as effective and carries less risk.

(http://www.physorg.com/news106418144.html)

Certainly, regular day-to-day use isn't a good idea, for your own health and the health of the wider environment. Anti-bacterials contain Triclosan. In August 2009 the Canadian Medical Association asked the Canadian government to ban Triclosan use in household products because of concerns with creating bacterial resistance and producing dangerous side products (chloroform). In the US, products containing Triclosan must declare this on the label.

For minor fresh cuts and wounds and for cleaning hands there are healthy natural alternatives. Always start with the obvious soap and water. Witchhazel is a good antiseptic. Buy in liquid form for cleaning up small cuts and grazes, dilute as necessary.

CHAPTER ELEVEN

A Healthy Bathroom

Everything – sinks, baths, shower screens and all hard surfaces can be cleaned with an E-cloth, as can blinds and curtains. If any stains refuse to shift, sprinkle Barkeepers Friend (from supermarkets) or borax over them and scrub. Use a scourer if the surface can take it. If not, use an ordinary (ie not E) cloth. Never use an E-cloth with cleaning chemical, it clogs up the microfibres and reduces its power to clean.

If the stain is really bad, make a paste with oxygen bleach powder, borax or Barkeepers Friend and lemon juice and leave it covering the mark for several hours or overnight.

For horizontal surfaces like a wall or a toilet, cover the paste with clingfilm and secure with a heavy duty adhesive tape. If any sticky residue is left from the tape adhesive, remove with WD40. Rinse WD40 thoroughly after use, especially on floors, as it makes surfaces very slippery.

A non-toxic product that will shift many difficult stains from hard surfaces and carpets (as well as stainless steel) is Quickleen-S Stainless Steel Cleaner (http://www.quickleen.co.uk)

my last resort stain remover of choice ever since it successfully removed dark hair dye stains from a wooden shelf.

Buy a large kitchen flour sprinkler and fill with borax powder to use as a daily toilet cleaner. Repackaging cleaning products like this doesn't tend to be necessary and should usually be avoided. It's essential to place a big, clear label of the contents firmly, and irremovably on the outside of the container before you even begin to think of filling it. Then, as with all cleaning products, store well away from children. Borax is hard to find in the shops but it's readily available online. I do run out from time to time and then use Ecover Toilet Cleaner. Don't forget to leave Ecover to sit for a while before you rinse. If you do use a toilet cleaner with nasty chemicals in it, avoid inhaling. This goes for oven and carpet cleaners as well.

If you see any limescale deposits building up (most commonly seen as that gunge that forms around the bases of taps), soak a kitchen towel in vinegar, cover the stain and leave overnight. Wipe off. To remove limescale from tap spouts, fill a small plastic bag with white vinegar. Place it over the spout so that the limescale is submerged in the vinegar. Secure the bag to the tap with an elastic band and leave for a few hours or overnight. If you don't like using plastic bags, cut 2 holes in each side of a paper cup, thread some string through and tie to the base of the tap.

Mould must be tackled immediately. If the stains are spotted early enough they'll come off with vinegar. If it's too late for that, dilute 2 parts warm water to 1 part chlorine bleach. Apply to the stain, leave for 15 minutes and rinse well. If the stain appears lighter, and only if the stain appears lighter, repeat until the mark has gone. You might have to keep at it over days, even weeks.

You could also try Astonish Mould and Mildew Remover (from supermarkets) or HG Hagesan Mould Spray (around £5.00/$8.09 from hardware stores). But again, don't give up too soon, and be prepared to reapply if necessary. Wear rubber gloves, follow all the maufacturer's instructions, and rinse the area thoroughly each time, especially between applications of bleach and any other product. If it's the sealant that's turning black, the marks can be cut out and the area resealed.

Find out what's causing the mould. Prevention is better than cure and ventilation is crucial. Opening a window for 10 minutes after a bath or shower will make all the difference. Keep furniture and wall cupboards away from external walls. Avoid carpets if possible.

When it comes to the contents of your bathroom cabinet, one tip I heard from several women at the cancer centre was to avoid deodorants containing parabens and aluminium. Cancer Research UK, however, says that there's no convincing evidence that antiperspirants and deodorants cause breast cancer and the whole scare was started by an email hoax. The charity Breakthrough Breastcancer says there's no evidence to suggest that deodorants, antiperspirants, aluminium salts, or shaving increase breast cancer risk. They quote a research project: "The largest study to date to investigate the issue examined the deodorant or antiperspirant use and underarm shaving habits of 813 women with breast cancer and 793 women with no history of the disease. There was no overall difference in deodorant and antiperspirant use and underarm shaving habits." The study was published in 2002 in the

Journal of the National Cancer Institute (JNCI).

There may not be any conclusive evidence but paraben-free and aluminium-free deodorants have now reached the High Street. All sorts of big brand 'Natural' antiperspirants with minerals and green packaging are also hitting the shelves, backed by major advertising campaigns. Quite an email hoax. Thankfully it's a personal choice. If you want to avoid parabens and aluminium, check the contents labels of all products, including those in green packaging, before buying. I keep a main brand antiperspirant for days when I think I might need it, but for day to day use I'll be sticking to my Weleda deodorant. It contains no aluminium or pthalates and uses natural ingredients to neutralise odour. Cancer Research UK points out that most modern deodorants are paraben-free now (so a move in the right direction then). I'll add, though, that the ingredients to look out for and avoid are: methylparaben, propylparaben, butylparaben, or benzylparaben.

Update: A few weeks ago Dr Philippa Darbre, Senior Lecturer in Oncology at the University of Reading, gave a speech at a friend's daughter's school. She talked a lot about parabens and cancer. It was, in fact, her research, back in 2004, that contributed to the debate about deodorants and breast cancer.

Her 2004 article *The Enemy Oestrogen* talks about unexplained high incidences of breast cancer in the upper outer quadrant of the breast with left breasts being more prone to cancer than the right. It also talks about a 2003 study which showed breast cancer diagnosis at an earlier age (as much as 22 years) in women who had used more deodorants/antiperspirants.

I contacted Professor Darbre to see if she was still concerned about parabens, oestrogen and the links between deodorants and breast cancer. Indeed she very much is. She sent me her paper: *Environmental Oestrogens and Breast Cancer: Evidence For Combined Involvement of Dietary, Household and Cosmetic Xenoestrogens*, written with Amelia K Charles and published in February 2010 by the Biomedical Sciences Section, School of Biological Sciences, University of Reading. They point out that cases of breast cancer in England & Wales have nearly doubled in the last 30 years. In 1979 there were 21,446 new cases, in 2006 there were 40,452. This works out at 84.5 cases for every 100,000 in the population in 1979 rising to 145.6 for every 100,000 in 2006. Most significantly, the rise in medullary, ductal or lobular tumors has risen from less than 10% in the 1970s to 75% at the end of the 1990s. 60% of all cases of breast cancer are due to ductal carcinomas. There is no proven link, this 'remains uncertain'. But, *"whilst cosmetic chemicals applied to the underarm and breast also need more research, the disproportionate incidence of breast cancer in the Upper Outer Quadrant is clarified"*. Professor Darbre doesn't underestimate the amount and complexity of the research that still needs to be done. In the meantime: *"the decision to apply oestrogenically active compounds in cosmetic products lies entirely with the user"*.

Dr Darbre is a patron of Cancer Active (http://www.canceractive.com/) a holistic cancer charity which provides information on orthodox, complimentary and alternative cancer therapies and treatments. Her online profile states: *The central role of oestrogen in breast cancer poses serious unanswered questions concerning the role of the many environmental chemicals which possess oestrogenic activity and which can enter the human breast. If exposure to complex mixtures of oestrogenic chemicals is a factor in breast cancer development, then a strategy for prevention of breast cancer might become a reality.*

(http://www.reading.ac.uk/biologicalsciences/about /staff/p-d-darbre.aspx)

Most researchers don't regard aluminium as a risk factor for Alzheimer's disease but there are theories that some people may be more at risk than others because their bodies have difficulty handling food containing copper, iron and aluminium. The contents of the bathroom cabinet is not my subject but it so happens that the publicist for this book has herself lived organically on a budget for many more years than I have. After reading through this chapter she told me about the mainstays of her bathroom cabinet. Though slightly off-subject, to make this, in every way, an organic home book I am now going to hand the rest of this chapter over to Emma Boden for some of her invaluable tips:

Like cleaning materials, public information on the ingredients in beauty products is still dubious. Animal testing for cosmetics is now banned in the UK and non-cosmetics testing is strictly controlled and regulated, but most medicines were probably at some point tested on animals. Nowadays, the majority of animals used in the UK for testing purposes are rats. Europe is not far behind on legislation but some countries have dragged their heels, despite widespread support from the public and scientists for controls across the continent. The US is even further behind but with powerful lobbyists such as PETA, the situation is improving.

For comprehensive information about animal testing in the UK visit (http://www.rspca.org.uk/home) which also covers EEC legislation. For the rest of the world, general information is pretty much up to date on (http://www.aboutanimaltesting.co.uk/).

A number of big brands already use humane, non-animal testing to ensure the safety of their products. As well as the many products found in your local health shop and in the organic sections of your supermarket, brands such as Body Shop are long term campaigners against animal testing and they focus on the use of natural as well as Fair Trade ingredients.

Beauty products don't have a sell-by date, this despite European Union rules stating that such products must carry advice on when they will expire. Some products such as 'out-of-date' mascara, foundation and concealer could be particularly hazardous, so use the same principles as you would with food: check by sight and by smell. Does the product look discoloured, do the ingredients appear to be separating or does it smell bad? In which case, throw it out! A general rule of thumb is to dispose of all cosmetics, including tanning and suncare products after a year.

Our skin is our body's largest organ and acts as our first line of defence against harmful substances, forming a finely tuned barrier which releases toxins (through perspiration for instance) but can also absorb them. We should therefore pay careful attention to what we put on our skin and this also applies to hair products and oral care products, which are absorbed even faster into the body via the mucous membrane. In this latter context, don't forget to look at your feminine hygiene products many of which contain potentially hazardous chemicals.

Try and avoid:

• *Sodium Laureth Sulfate/Sodium Lauryl Sulfate (SLS), also used to dissolve grease in car engines, seems to be added in one of its forms to just about everything including toothpastes, beauty and bath products and a huge number of household ranges. Simply put, its main purpose is to help produce bubbles, which we have come to think of as cleansing, although the opposite is closer to the truth. SLS breaks down fats (not in a healthy way!) and impairs the skin's ability to absorb moisture. Even more worryingly it's classified as a mutagen, which means it can alter genetic material in cells.*

• *Benzaldehyde affects the central nervous system, can make you feel dizzy and nauseous as well as provoking sudden drops in blood pressure if inhaled.*

• *Benzyl Acetate. The US Environmental Working Group's cosmetic safety database (http://www.ewg.org/skindeep) indicates that research studies have found it to be carcinogenic. It can also have an adverse effect on your respiratory system and eyesight.*

• *Parabens, once considered safe, are used as a preservative in a huge number of products and have recently been re-implicated in the cancer debate.*

• Petroleum based products (in skin care and first aid) interfere with the skin's ability to absorb oxygen (ironically part of the natural healing process). Rather than moisturise, as intended, these creams dehydrate and can irritate. There is also evidence of them containing micro-particles of 1,4-dioxane, a known animal and probable human carcinogen.

When it comes to perfumes, the smaller boutique perfumes are generally cleaner than the big brands, which is why they can be so expensive. It's also why they evaporate so much faster than those invasive mass market smells. For best value perfume use single note scents which can be very clean, eg Lily, Violet, Rose etc. The cleanest will come from a herbalist or natural health store. Rose water makes a good toner and is particularly reasonable if you buy a good quality version destined for cooking. Similarly good food grade virgin coconut oil is a great alternative moisturiser (skin and hair) and also has great healing properties thanks to its antibacterial, antioxidant and antifungal properties. Use witchhazel for zapping spots.

For scented baths, use readily available herbs (for instance lavender or rosemary) in a muslin cloth strung over the tap or tied and dropped into the bath. Or add a couple of drops of your favourite essential oil mixed with almond oil which helps diffuse the oil into water. Tea Tree Essential oil (take care to dilute as particularly strong) in the bath is good for fungal infections and lavender is very effective as an antibacterial and an antifungal and smells a great deal pleasanter than Tea Tree.

*Your local independent health store is the perfect place to do some research. Many independents, such as Olivers (*http://www.oliverswholefoods.co.uk/*) in London have skin care and other qualified health care experts working in their shops – a good chance to pick up some free professional advice if you go in on the right day. Since it's my local health store I also happen to know that they price check local supermarkets to make sure they are competitive on as many products as possible. And don't forget the good old The Body Shop which is very good for affordable Glycerine-based soaps as well as healthy products for the boys and girls in your life.*

Thanks Emma. This could fill another book – perhaps *will* be another book one day.

*In the meantime, read the labels and check products on a reliable website. I found (*http://www.safecosmetics.co.uk/*) to be a very good general resource on cosmetic safety in the UK, and (*http://www.theremustbeabetterway.co.uk/*) is particularly good for products and information on skincare. Another excellent online source for well-priced 'chemical' free products is (http://www.red23.co.uk/). Type your postcode into the Weleda website to find your nearest stockist of their natural, cruelty free bodycare products or buy online at(http://www.weleda.co.uk/).*

*In the US, (*http://bodyecology.com/*) takes an intelligent look at the use of toxic products that can affect your immune system along with practical solutions for improving your wellbeing. For more information in the US check the Good Guide, (*http://www.goodguide.com/*) which keeps up to date with all the latest environmental and health information on* *beauty products, household chemicals, food and plastics.*

CHAPTER TWELVE

Are You Getting The Most Out Of Your Household Contents Insurance?

When you're renewing your household insurance policy or taking out a new one, have a close look at the accidental damage section. What's included and not included varies widely from company to company. If a leak comes through your ceiling onto your duvet, for example, some companies will pay out for a new duvet, others won't. If one curtain is ruined beyond saving, some companies will replace a whole set of curtains to match the damaged one, irrespective of how many are in the set, others will only replace the match in the pair, others won't replace any at all. Some companies will replace new for new. For example, even if only one chair is damaged, they'll replace the whole suite so that everything matches, or it could be a piece of jewellery, like an ear-ring, to match exactly. Others will only pay out on items like DVD players, TVs and window glass.

If you do have a catastrophic spill, don't, like so many, forget that you might be covered. So many people are afraid to claim on their household contents insurance, worried that they'll lose their 'no claims bonus'. It's not like cars. If your insurance company does decide you're more of a risk and puts your premiums up, switch to another one.

Changing your insurer, and seeing what's included

and not included in the small print, is much simpler than it used to be. It really is worth making a note of your annual renewal date, especially if you pay by direct debit, and check what you could be saving, or which deals, like comprehensive accidental damage, could be added, by switching insurers. You only have to fill out your details once to receive dozens of quotes. I've just renewed my annual car insurance online – with the same company. Beating their renewal quote sent to me in the post by £40.00 ($62.50). Look for links that earn you instant cashbacks of £25.00 ($38) and more. Just click through to the comparison site and the free cash will be sent to you. Generally this happens when the insurance has been in place for 60 days so you have to make a note on your calendar to send in an email claim.

UK reader can go to the Moneysavingexpert insurance pages to find their latest recommendation for comparison sites. This fantastic independent, advertisement-free site is one of the biggest consumer success stories of the internet.

(http://www.moneysavingexpert.com)

CHAPTER THIRTEEN

Help! Over 100 Readers' Cleaning and Stains Catastrophes Solved

Before becoming a writer I was a researcher at the BBC where I wrote and produced a couple of my own documentaries for the Arts Department. The importance of clarity, accuracy and integrity was hammered into us. If I'm not 100% sure about the right way to go about answering a question I'll find an expert who is. Over the years I've built up quite a database of these, many of whom are open to online queries free of charge. I give the links to these at the end of the book. But first, here are some of the trickiest dilemmas I have been set over the years.

Because these columns were published for a British newspaper, commercial products mentioned are not always available outside the UK. Natural, universal remedies are given wherever possible. Websites must be consulted for information on inclusiveness or not of VAT, postage and packing and whether international shipping is available. Details of good places to buy natural, non-commercial products can be found in Chapter Two – What About The Vinegar.

My dishwasher smells really bad for about five minutes when I turn it on. The smell comes up from the plughole in the sink. Help!

First check your plumbing. To prevent the odours coming up through the plughole, the drain hose from the dishwasher must be connected below the u-bend trap of the sink. Sometimes the drain hose can get dislodged, especially if the cupboard under your sink is full of clutter. Check also for water leakage at the point where the drain hose meets the sink waste pipe and tighten the locking sleeve if necessary. Also check to see if you have a dirty u-bend. It's possible that the surge of hot water is sending the smell up through the plug. Push a plumber's wire down the plughole to stir up any sediment, then pour down a cup of baking soda or half a cup of Soda Crystals. Leave for 10 minutes and then flush with hot water. For general dishwasher freshness, clean out the system every so often by placing a mug of white vinegar (or brown if you don't have white) on the bottom shelf and running on empty for a short glass-washing cycle.

How do you get rust spots off a stainless-steel fridge? There are streaks of ingrained grime. I've tried several stainless-steel cleaners without success. Help!

Make a paste of cream of tartar (from the baking section of supermarkets) and lemon juice, apply, leave for an hour or so, then rub off. Repeat if necessary. Ingrained grime on brushed stainless steel can be cleaned off with a little baby oil. For general cleaning, wipe over with a slightly damp E-cloth or vinegar on a damp cloth. The best commercial stainless-steel cleaner

I've come across is Quickleen-S. Only available online, (around £10.00/$16.19 www.quickleen.co.uk).

Quickleen-S is a nontoxic cleaner that you can use all around the home, both inside and out. Phosphorous-free, odourless and food-safe, it removes rust and a variety of stubborn stains. Apply with a wet cloth, rub away the stains and wipe dry immediately. Another option is Barkeepers Friend (from hardware stores and supermarkets). It isn't as powerful but is a lot cheaper and good for general cleaning. Sprinkle on to a wet cloth, rub gently and rinse. For stubborn stains make a paste, apply, remove after a minute and rinse. Don't use on mirror-polished stainless steel.

Our cats are refusing to use their litter tray and wee on the carpet. How can I clean it and how do I stop them? Help!

It could be because they don't like sharing a litter tray – try giving them their own trays in their own territories. But there are so many other possible causes, you'd have to work through one of the countless cat psychology books available. Vicky Halls' Cat Detective or Cat Confidential come recommended (Bantam Press). There are almost as many stain-removal and deterrent tips as there are cat books: lemon juice, vinegar, baking soda, borax, tea tree oil, onion, silver foil, plastic bags or putting scratching posts near the stained spots are just a few. Don't use strong-smelling chemicals, especially white vinegar or ammonia, because they may make the area more attractive to your cat. Hot water and steam cleaners should also be avoided because heat will set the odour. Keep a bottle of soda water for light, fresh marks; keep blotting and reapplying. For older stains, dilute some biological detergent in lukewarm water, froth up and dab with the foam. To get rid of any chemical residue that will react with the proteins in the urine – this is what makes a cat return to the same spot – use an odour neutraliser. Safe4 Odour Killer (around £4.00/$6.48, http://www.petremedies.co.uk) is a blend of organic oils that eliminates strong animal odours, and other smells such as cigarette smoke. Or hire a wet-vac, which will force clean water through the carpet. If a cat has a seriously distressing, furniture-damaging medical problem to do with its bottom end, you can buy nappies for it at (http://www.dog-nappy.co.uk/).

Our lava lamp has smashed. Goo has gone all over our carpet and dried like a white emulsion. I've tried everything but nothing works. Help!

This a nasty combination stain, probably consisting of wax, oil, alcohol and dye. The exact make up of the liquid inside lava lamps has been a trade secret since they were invented in the 60s, but the main ingredients are believed to be wax and carbon tetrachloride, a toxic chemical once widely used as a pesticide and dry-cleaning solvent. If your lamp was made before the mid-80s, treat the stain with caution, and wear gloves and a face mask when working on it. First, fill a bag with ice and place it over the stain for several hours. Hopefully the emulsion you describe will turn out to be wax, which will harden. Carefully pick off as much as you can with a blunt metal object such as an old palette knife or screwdriver. Cover what's left with white blotting paper and carefully apply a warm (not hot) iron in short bursts until all the wax has melted into the blotting paper. You'll be left with a greasy dye stain. Dab with neat methylated spirits, rinse, then wash with a non-toxic carpet shampoo such as Earth Friendly Carpet Shampooo around £6.50 / $10.53 (http://www.auravita.com/product/Earth-Friendly-Carpet-Shampoo.EAFR10005.html?RefId=220&adid=EAFR 10005) – made with fresh scented bergamot and sage, it cleans just as well as conventional brands and is Peta- (People for the Ethical Treatment of Animals) approved.

I want to clean my sheepskin rug but, at 2m x 1.5m it's too big for my washing machine. The natural pile is about 8cm which seems too shallow for Vax-type appliances. Help!

Boil 200g of soap flakes and three tablespoons of olive oil in one litre of water. Mix and add to a bath of warm water. Alternatively, use a teaspoon of baby shampoo or a mild liquid wool detergent, such as Ecover Delicate Wool Wash (around £3.50/$5.67 from supermarkets and hardware stores). Never use biological detergent, bleach or fabric softeners. Give the rug a vigorous shake before immersing it in the water, hairy side down. Wash thoroughly and rinse. Squeeze out as much excess water as you can and dab both sides with a clean white towel. Pull gently back into shape and brush the damp wool in one direction with a wire brush a dog-grooming brush is ideal. Hang outside on a washing line or lay flat to dry. Brush several times over the next few days. Avoid any sort of heat throughout: hot water, airing cupboards, sunlight, tumble dryers, radiators, fan heaters.

Leaky timber cladding has left us with a dark tidemark at the end of one of the original beams high up in our converted barn. Now I'm left with water stains on the wood. Help!

Many stains on wood can be removed by sanding, but water stains can be stubborn. You could try scrubbing with soap and water, but you'd have to go over the whole beam, and you may find the tidemark is still visible afterwards. Building expert John Oxley, from Construction Chemicals, says that if, as is likely, the stain has been caused by water extracting the tannins from the timber, it can be removed with oxalic acid. Initially, the wood may appear lighter where it has been treated, but it will eventually merge with the rest of the beam. Oxalic acid is poisonous and extremely dangerous, so follow any application and safety instructions rigidly. If you've not used it before, buy the acid combined with a safety kit (around £30.00/$48.40 http://constructionchemicals.co.uk). If you have any queries, email sales@constructionchemicals.co.uk.

The books in my library have a fine brown powder on them which leaves round spots. There's an obvious mouldy smell but in the drier places I can see dust. There are also small brown spots on some of my pieces of wooden furniture and curtains in other rooms. Help!

I spoke to paper conservation and restoration expert, Graham Bignell. 'All the signs point to a damp or airless environment creating moulds,' he says. 'Mould spores, once active in the right environment, flourish and spread, and things that appear dry to the eye may be damp enough for mould to grow. Once you have that environment, it will inevitably attract damp-loving insect pests, so it is vital to improve air circulation and reduce humidity. Bignell says he would need more details to be specific. To find a book conservator in your area, consult the Conservation Register:

(http://www.conservationregister.com/index.asp),

a national register of accredited experts in books, ceramics, clocks, furniture, paintings, musical instruments, sculpture, stained glass, textiles and more. You'll also find guidance on choosing and working with a conservator, plus tips on caring for books, art, antiques and the decorative features of buildings.

On a trip to China I bought a duvet filled with thin layers of silk. It's very light and warm and we use it in summer and in winter. I was told the lining mustn't be dry-cleaned or washed but the cotton covers could be taken off for washing. I'm scared to do this in case I destroy the filling. Help!

The best silk duvets are made with silk harvested from silkworms fed on mulberry leaves. Hundreds of layers are hand-woven together, making strong and durable fillings, with removable covers. Pure Silk Duvets range in price from £90/ $144.00 for a lightweight single to £225/$360 for a super king (http://www.puresilkduvet.com/). The cheapest are made from scraps of silk bundled together in a casing that will lose shape or even fall apart if you remove the cover. Silk duvets mustn't be washed in their entirety or dry-cleaned. They are naturally hypoallergenic and resistant to dust mites, and normally all you need to do is hang them out in warm, not hot, sunlight for an hour or so several times a year. If in doubt about removing your cover, don't. In future, use the duvet as you would a blanket – with sheets, or with your own duvet cover. Spot-treat any obvious stains and marks with Tenestar, which is specifically designed for washing pure silk, silk mixtures and viscose (from some hardware stores, or around £6.00/$9.72 http://www.sulis.co.uk). If the duvet is heavily soiled, find a local dry-cleaner who can advise on the new 'wet cleaning' process. This is a non-toxic, environmentally safe alternative to dry-cleaning, and may well be suitable for your silk duvet.

The white tiles on my black and white chequered porch floor have ingrained dirt. The house was built in 1888. Help!

The gentlest method would be to mix a thick paste of either bicarbonate of soda, oxygen bleach or borax with water. Spread over tiles and rub in with a damp cloth. Leave for several hours, then scrub off. The dirt could well be so ingrained, though, that you'll need something stronger. Aqua Mix Sealer & Coating Remover is a non-flammable, multipurpose stripper that dissolves deep-set stains from natural stone, ceramic, porcelain, grout, quarry, Saltillo, terracotta, cement and masonry (from hardware and tile stores, or appx £18.00/$29.16 http://www.amazon.co.uk). Wear protective clothing and follow all safety instructions. Remove & Go is another multipurpose stripper formulated with a long dwell-time to remove most ingrained stains from ceramic tiles. (Around £17.00/$27.54 from tile shops.)

We have heat marks on the walls above our radiators. We're about to redecorate. How can we stop this happening again. Help!

Before you redecorate, paint over the existing marks with Polycell Stain Stop, which covers soot, rust, water stains, grease, nicotine and crayon on plaster, masonry and wood (from hardware stores appx £7.00/$11.34). You may need two coats. To help prevent the marks reappearing, don't let the dust that gathers behind all the little grooves and fins at the back of the radiators layer up. Vacuum as regularly as you do other surfaces and every so often push a babywipe or microfibre cloth down through the grooves on a cane. A hard-wearing eco paint will make it easier to clean off marks. Ecos Organic Paint is odourless and solvent free and totally free of all pesticides, herbicides and toxins.

I have just bought a secondhand chest of drawers but it reeks of tobacco. I've tried washing all the inner parts, rubbing with lemon juice, and I've also tried leaving perfumed soap in the drawers but they still stink. Help!

Vinegar, baking soda, borax and activated charcoal are all natural smell-absorbers. Sprinkle or place in bowls inside the drawers, or, better still, make a thick paste of baking soda or borax and water, smear this over the wood inside and out, and leave for 24 hours. Buy activated charcoal from aquarium shops (ask for Eheim Ehfikarbon) and place a small bowl in each drawer.

I live on a narrowboat and have lots of little black stains, spider poo, on the curtains. I'd hate to poison them. Help!

Reduce their food source by cleaning away bugs as soon as they appear, and use a humane barrier spray such as No More Spiders (Around £7.80/$12.63 http://www.diypcs.co.uk/acatalog/no-more-spiders.html). Spray around doors, windows, wherever the spiders get into your boat. The natural chestnut extract and clover leaf oil prevents them entering the protected area without harming them. Ultrasonic spider repellents don't have a great track record. These look a little like air-freshener plugs. When plugged in, they emit a high-pitched sound, too high for humans and pets (other than rodents and insects) to hear. Ultrasonic waves are like ordinary light waves in that they don't penetrate solid objects such as walls and cupboards so they work only in the room where the device is plugged in. Better, go for an electromagnetic repeller. This sends electric pulses throughout the wiring of a house (or boat). They're thought to affect the nervous systems of spiders, driving them away. The combined ultrasonic and electromagnetic Pest Stop/Pest Clear 3000 Spider Repeller works on spaces up to 3,000 sq ft and is suitable for treating infestations (around £47.00/$76.13 http://www.pesthelp.co.uk/weshop/Spiders.asp).

My plastic shower tray has gone yellow around the edges. I want something that'll bring it back to its original white. Help!

The staining may be irreversible, but scrubbing with toilet cleaner is worth a try. Or mix two scoops of powdered oxygen bleach with one scoop of warm water, rub the paste into the stains, leave for half an hour, then rinse off. Don't let it come into contact with wood, lacquered, varnished or silk surfaces, or mild steel. Or, use the same approach with Barkeepers Friend but keep away from enamel baths and surfaces. Another possibility is 3% hydrogen peroxide solution (around £1.00/$1/62 from the pharmacy) which is normally used to bleach hair, paper, teeth, bones and plastic. It's non-toxic, biodegradable and a far closer relative to water than chlorine bleach, its chemical structure being just one oxygen atom away. Handle with care, though, and follow the storage instructions because it's highly flammable. It's also highly corrosive to metal, so keep away from taps and bathroom fittings. Sponge stains and leave for several hours or overnight.

One of our kids has smeared Vaseline on the painted wall, I can't shift it. Help!

Try the ultimate greasy stain remover: washing-up liquid. Dab a little neat, colourless liquid such as Ecover Washing Up Liquid onto the stain and dab gently with a damp cloth. If this doesn't work, try either Sticky Stuff Remover (£4.99, from hardware stores or supermarkets), a Magic Eraser Block (Around £4.00/£6.48 http://www.lakeland.co.uk) or Zam sponge erasers (£1.00/$1.61 from Poundland). Eraser blocks are soft, smooth, non-abrasive cleaning sponges. When damp, the microscopic fibres develop an eraser-like quality, shifting stains from many surfaces without the need for chemicals or detergents. As well as getting those finger- and scuff marks off walls, they'll remove stains off cups and burned-on food from cookware.

Our kitchen floor tiles are rough, matt, large farmhouse-type. They're hard to clean and get dirty very quickly. Would steam cleaning work? Help!

'From your description, these are probably of a flagstone variety,' says the Tile Doctor. 'They're similar to sandstone, but with a much rougher texture that, as you've discovered, shreds mops and makes them very difficult to clean. Hire a buffing machine and ask for it to be fitted with a scrub board attachment rather than a buffing pad. Mix three parts warm water with one part Tile Doctor Pro-Clean, (Around £12.00 http://www.tiledoctor.co.uk). Pour a quantity of this on to the flag floor and scrub away. Pro-Clean is a powerful, multipurpose high-alkaline cleaner, stripper and degreaser. Avoid all skin contact and wear rubber gloves and eye protection.' Larger DIY stores such as Homebase have hire sections, and most will deliver and collect equipment. The cost will be about £30.00/$48.60 a day, but check weekend fees, which may be a little more. Then, once the floor is clean, rinse it all over with cold water. When it's completely dry, apply five coats of Tile Doctor Seal And Go Sealer (Around £15.00/$24.30) or Liberon Stone Floor Sealer (Around £13.00 /$21.06 http://www.partridgeshadleigh.co.uk/catalog). The best way to do this easily and quickly is to use a paint pad on a pole attachment. Leave each coat to dry in between sealing – give each coat about 30 minutes at room temperature. Some floor cleaners could damage the sheen on the sealer. Check that it's a pH-neutral tile cleaner such as Tile Doctor Neutral Tile Cleaner (Around £11.00), or Aqua Mix Concentrated Stone And Tile Cleaner (from hardware stores). For regular cleaning, the best tool to invest in would be a Wet Vax machine, which you can also use to wet-clean carpets. The cheapest costs about £95.00/$153.90 on eBay.

I've got melted carpet on the bottom of my (very good) iron. How do I clean it off? Help!

The old-fashioned method was to wipe over the hot

base with a bar of soap, then rub with a towel when cool enough to touch. Another was to smear on a paste of salt and vinegar, and scrub with a scourer. Modern coatings wouldn't respond well to these treatments, however, and unless your iron is ancient, they're best avoided. Faultless Hot Iron Cleaner (Around £6.00/$9.72   http://www.lakeland.co.uk/7260/Hot-Iron-Cleaner) is a cream cleaner that's safe for use on all metal, Teflon- and Silverstone-coated soleplates. It's more expensive than other iron cleaners but does come recommended. For best results apply with an old face cloth or bath towel.

How do I clean my white granite kitchen sink? The manufacturer's guidelines say that scrubbing is enough and not to use bleach or products containing bleach. But it isn't working. Help!

Modern granite sinks aren't necessarily hewn out of hunks of solid granite. Often, they're made of crushed, or 'near', granite, and care and maintenance will depend on the type you have. For general cleaning, sink specialists Sinks-taps recommend Barkeepers Friend. Sprinkle on to the sink, scrub into a paste with a stiff, nylon, short-stubble nail brush, then rinse off. Sinks-taps can't guarantee that this would work best, however, unless they know the manufacturer. Email website@sinks-taps.com, and they'll be happy to advise you further. For general, everyday cleaning without having recourse to any detergents at all use an E-cloth. E-Cloth's washing-up pad cuts through grease and grime (Around £3.00/$4/86 http://www.e-cloth.com/products/kitchen/).

When my husband varnished our pine kitchen

work surfaces some of the varnish got left behind on our white wall tiles and we can't get it off. Help!

Home Strip Paint And Varnish Remover (Around £7.00/$11.34 http://www.decoratingdirect.co.uk/ or hardware stores) is a new water-based stripper that's much safer for the environment and easier to use than solvent-based varieties. Non-flammable, biodegradable and non-corrosive, it's suitable for all types of stone, brick, wood, metal, marble, glass and reinforced plastics. It doesn't give off nasty fumes. Try a small test area first, then apply liberally. Leave it to penetrate for 30 minutes, then peel away the varnish with a scraper.

Our Christmas tree was lodged onto a log slice this year. Now we've taken it down there's a big stain on our light-coloured carpet that won't come off. Help!

There are several methods you can try – with care. Always test on a hidden part of the carpet first; work from the outside of the stain in and always use a clean, white cloth or white paper towels. In a bowl of lukewarm water, whoosh up a scoop of biological washing powder until there's a layer of foam on the top. Apply the foam to the stain using short, light rubbing movements. Rinse by dabbing with lukewarm water. If this doesn't work, try damping a cloth with turpentine. Press over the stain and apply gentle pressure. Turpentine is smelly and greasy, so open windows, wear gloves and don't pour directly on to the stain – it could damage the carpet backing. As the stain lifts, move to a clean, dampened part of the cloth. Rinse well by dabbing with lukewarm water.

Black enamel is building up a skin of unsightly

grunge around the cast-iron hobs of my Rayburn cooker. I know I can't use anything abrasive, I've already tried Aga hob cleaner but the marks are still there. Help!

Rayburns are coated with vitreous enamel which is, in effect, glass, fused to metal at a very high temperature. It's incredibly durable, hygienic and easy to clean but you are right to be cautious because it can be damaged beyond repair if you use the wrong cleaner or abrasive. IVE and the VEA (Institute of Vitreous Enamellers and Vitreous Enamel Association) carries out strict tests on cleaners and those that pass have the VEA's approval printed clearly on the pack. Most of the Cif, Flash and Astonish range are OK for everyday cleaning but before selecting a product or fragrance you haven't used before, always check for the IVE VEA logo. Of the tougher cleaners, Oven Mate Oven, Grill, Pan and Barbecue Cleaner and Astonish Grime Blast Enamel Cream are safe to use but Tableau Carbon Remover is probably your best bet. From some hardware stores, see

(http://www.iom3.org/content/vitreous-enamel).

Ideal for vitreous enamel, it's a non-caustic gel that you brush on, leave overnight and rinse off. It can be used on all metals, glass, porcelain and ceramics. Liquids boiling over on to the hotplate aren't a problem, but milk or fruit juice spills could cause permanent damage – wipe immediately. Don't use cold, wet cloths. For more advice, go to (http://rayburn-web.co.uk/homepage.aspx).

A child got hold of the gloves I use for carrying coal and has left palm prints all over my double-glazed windows. Now I can't get rid of them in any

way. Help!

It must be the rubber from the glove that has melded the sooty stains to the glass. A spray of WD-40 is worth a go. If that doesn't work, Goo Gone probably will (Around £6.70/$10.85

http://www.axminster.co.uk/goo-gone-prod376969/?searchfor=goo%20gone). This cult American product is a powerful, citrus-based, non-toxic sticky stuff remover that gets rid of gum, tree sap, asphalt, wax and a host of other difficult marks from all sorts of surfaces, including glass (as long as it's not tinted). Some vets apparently use it to get tar off pets and wild birds. Apply to the stains and leave to penetrate, but don't let it dry out. If the marks don't budge, reapply. Hopefully it will eventually dissolve everything into a horrible, smeary mess. Wipe this off with a second application of Goo Gone and a clean, white cloth. The professional option is Oil-Flo 141 (Around £8.40/$13.60

http://www.windowcleancentre.co.uk/productdetails.aspx?ProductID=184).

Biodegradable and nonflammable, it's specially formulated to dissolve numerous adhesives, including tar, silicone sealant and graffiti, from glass and other hard surfaces.

I have a settee with hairspray stains that are ingrained into the green leather. Help!

They may be impossible to remove. It depends how deep they go and the type of leather. Dull, matt finishes are particularly difficult to treat. There are a few things you can try but remember always to test on a hidden area of the sofa first. Some greasy stains can be removed with a mild solution of washing-up liquid and warm water: apply, leave for a few minutes, then wipe off. Or cover the stain with a thin layer of adhesive from a bike puncture repair kit. Leave it to dry overnight, then gently peel away. If it has left a dry patch on your testing area, rub a little Vaseline Petroleum Jelly (around £1.00/$1.62 from the pharmacy) into the leather to see if that brings it back to its original texture. One product that might work is White Wizard (Around £5.00/$8.10 http://www.lakeland.co.uk) an odourless spread-on/wipe-off stain-removing cream.

My old thatched cottage has a very large fireplace. After many years of fires, the granite has black, tarry deposits. I've now got a woodburner and want to clean it away. Help!

I asked master stonemason Colin Yates of Conserv at Stone Tech (Cleveland) Ltd (http://www.lime-mortars.co.uk/). "Assuming the fireplace is built from unpolished granite and not made of another stone with granite components, I'd recommend a high-powered stone degreaser kit." Universeal Stone Cleaner (Around £14.00/$22.68) is a heavy duty cleaner suitable for cleaning all types of natural stone, including sandstone, limestone & polished marble. It is environmentally friendly and easily cleans the toughest stains & heavy soiling. 'Apply by brush and leave for 10 minutes before applying a second coat,' Yates says. 'Then, in one direction only, rub with an abrasive pad. Once a lather has been achieved and the smoke begins to lift from the surface, the stone can be rinsed with an old sponge and clean water. Leave to dry and apply further coats, rubbing with the pad until the stone becomes clean. The finished surface should be sealed with an invisible water-based sealer such as NoStain Natura (Around £25.00/$40.50), which does not change the appearance or colour of the stone and is invisible once dry. This will help maintain and protect the granite.' For advice on cleaning polished granite and other stone surfaces, email the Conserv helpline info@conserv.uk.net.

Our son is a smoker. Now he's going away we've replaced the carpet in his room with wooden floors and the curtains with blinds but it still stinks of smoke. Help!

White vinegar, borax, bicarbonate of soda, activated charcoal and ammonia are all natural odour removers. Wearing rubber gloves, wipe down all hard surfaces with a cloth dampened in hot water and sprinkled with borax or bicarbonate of soda. Alternatively, if there are no varnished, lacquered or aluminium surfaces, mix one cup of white vinegar and one cup of washing Soda Crystals (from supermarkets) with one pint of boiling water and a few drops of essential oil, preferably citrus like Lemon Essential Oil (Around £3.00/$4.86 http://www.holisticshop.co.uk or pharmacies). If the smell persists, leave a few bowls of ammonia in the room overnight and close the door. Ammonia is poisonous and should be used only as a last resort. Don't use if you have pets. Wear a mask when retrieving the bowls and open the windows for several hours. Safer alternatives are bowls of activated charcoal, vinegar or baking soda.

The keys of my 1996 Steinway grand piano are dirty and need cleaning. I want to do this without damaging the instrument? Help!

Modern Steinway piano keys are made of a synthetic ivory substitute called Ivorene. Wipe with a clean piece of cheesecloth or E-cloth, lightly dampened, being careful that no moisture seeps between the keys – dampness in the keybed can cause swelling. If a more thorough clean is required, piano retailer and restorer Kensington & Chelsea Pianos suggests an eco window cleaner which contains vinegar, such as Earth Friendly Window Kleener with Vinegar (around £3.50/$5.67

http://www.biggreensmile.com). Dampen a clean piece of cheesecloth and wipe on to the keys.

Alternatively, Cory Key Brite (Around £7.00/$11.34 http://www.pianoaccessoryshop.co.uk) cleans and preserves plastic and ivory keys.

I have been given an old set of Le Creuset saucepans. The insides have been cleaned with a scouring compound or bleach so the smooth finish of the enamel has become rough to touch. Can chemicals leach from the enamel into food? Do I need to get them resurfaced? Can this be done? Help!

I spoke to Le Creuset who said the pans are totally safe to use. 'We don't offer a resurfacing service and haven't heard of it being done anywhere. Our Le Creuset Pots & Pans Cleaner (Around £6.50/$10.53 from kitchen shops) cleans cream enamel inside and out but isn't suitable for nonstick surfaces. To remove long-term staining on any of our pans, we recommend that you put 2 tbsp of biological powder into the pan with cold water. Bring to a boil on a medium heat hob, leave for a couple of minutes to froth up, then clean out with a nylon scourer.'

I have two china casseroles that have jammed together, one's at an angle inside the other. I've tried leverage, heat, cold and soapy water all without success. I'd sacrifice the inner dish if necessary. Help!

You've got to get enough of a temperature differential between the two by directing cold and heat as appropriate. Fill the smaller one with ice and leave it for a few hours so that the coldness penetrates the china. Then gradually warm up the outer casserole with a hairdryer. Hopefully the heat will expand the larger one more than the smaller one so that they can be prised apart.

My old cast-iron bath needs a good clean. It's really grimy with rust around the taps. Can I use a borax paste on enamel? Help!

Borax is very enamel friendly. Sprinkled on to a damp cloth, it removes stains from baths, tiles, sinks, drains, floors, windows, mirrors and painted surfaces, eliminates odours and acts as an antifungal. It can also be mixed with bleach and other (non-acidic) cleaning products to enhance their cleaning power. Smear the stains on your bath with a thick paste of borax and lemon juice, leave overnight and scrub off with a scourer or nailbrush. To get rid of light rust marks, rub with half a lemon sprinkled with salt. For more stubborn rust stains, mix a paste of cream of tartar (Around £1.00/$1.62 from supermarket baking sections) and 3% hydrogen peroxide solution (Around £1.00/$1.62 from pharmacies) leave for an hour or so and scrub off. Don't use chlorine bleach, which sets rust stains. A damp pumice stone will also remove rust from most surfaces (don't use on metal or aluminium). If you use a commercial rust remover, follow safety instructions very carefully as they contain poisonous acids. To repair any chips and flaking, use Cramer Scratch and Chip Repair Kit (Around £19.00/$30.78 from http://www.plumbworld.co.uk).

Our new deep-pile rug is shedding a lot. It's pure wool. I gather you can stop angora wool jumpers moulting by putting them in the freezer. Is it safe to do this with my rug? Would it work? Help!

It's normal for new wool rugs and carpets to shed for the first few months, but yes, some rug experts do advise freezing as a way of stopping this. As long as your rug is made from 100% wool (or any other animal fibre) and will fit in the freezer without crumpling, roll or fold it into four, place in a plastic bag and leave in the freezer for 24 hours. Freezing also destroys moth grubs in woollen carpets and jumpers, though you have to leave them for a longer time, two weeks to be sure, and follow with a professional clean. Great care must be taken when thawing. Hang the rug somewhere such as a bathroom, safely away from other carpets and wooden floors. Damp can lead to rot and mildew, so make sure it's completely dry before re-laying or vacuuming.

I've got candle wax drips all over my marble fireplace. Help!

The easiest way to remove the wax drips is to melt them gently away with a warm hairdryer. Have a paper towel ready to dab up the wax as it softens. Then use a gentle cleaner such as Lithofin Easy-Clean Spray (Around £9.00/$14.58 from hardware stores) which dissolves surface dirt and greasy deposits from marble, granite, limestone and artificial stone. It's very simple to use, leaves no streaks and has a pleasant odour. Tikko Stone Soap is another good option (Around £10.00/$16.19 from tile shops). Once the marble is clean and shiny, regular wipes with an E-cloth will keep it that way. If the fireplace is very badly stained, Lithofin Stain-Away Special Remover (Around £20.00/$32.40 from Pure Adhesion, as before) is a strong cleaner thick enough to be used on vertical surfaces. It will dissolve hardened wax, sealants, oil, grease, paint, lacquer and bitumen. Handle with care and follow all safety instructions.

I have an old cream sofa that's covered with food and hand-mark stains. We've had them cleaned but the marks haven't come out. They've been Scotchguard protected. Help!

It sounds like you've got a mixture of protein stains (most foodstuffs), tannin stains (juice, tea, coffee) and probably some dye stains as well. Because heat sets protein stains, and soap sets tannin stains, these should have been spot-treated separately before the covers were washed. Some may now have set permanently. Glycerine (about £2.00/$3.24 from pharmacies) works well on old stains, and even gets rid of old red wine stains. Moisten with cold water and rub the Glycerine in with a finger. Repeat. If the stain is fading, keep at it over a few days. Dye pigment is particularly difficult to remove. After colour testing, spot-treat with a clean, white cloth dipped in methylated spirits or, better still, mix equal parts of methylated spirits and ammonia together (one of the rare times when you can mix ammonia with anything) and dab at the stains. If you're using ammonia, ventilate the room well, wear a mask and make sure all children and pets are very far away. Rinse thoroughly. For tea, coffee, beer, tannin, water marks and other yellow and brown discolorations, as you've already used silicone-based Scotchgard, you'll need to use a solvent-based product. Try Prochem's Coffee Stain Remover (around £5.50/$8.91 http://www.windowcleaningstuff.co.uk).

I have a patio covered with worn, dull-looking grey slate. I want to restore it to a highly polished sheen. Help!

'As the surface is outside, liquid polishes or internal slate sealers can't be used,' said natural stone flooring expert Helen Kirk, of Stone Floors Direct (http://www.stonefloorsdirect.co.uk)'An exterior pavement sealer would brighten the stone, but it wouldn't be long before the exposed stone reacted to the atmosphere and lost its shine again. To achieve the long-lasting, highly polished sheen you're after, you would have to hire a professional to steam-clean the slate and finish it off with a polishing machine. It would then stay looking good for two to three years, which, in the long term, would give the best and most economical result.' To find a reputable slate polisher in your area, type your postcode and 'slate' into the Guild of Master Craftsmen's database (http://www.findacraftsman.com/).

My husband has made a kitchen work surface spray using methylated spirits which he says is the best way to get rid of grease. Help!

Methylated spirits are smelly, toxic and highly flammable, and so it's definitely not a good idea to use them on kitchen surfaces. Instead of using meths to get rid of the grease marks and stains, tell your husband that for day to day cleaning, you need nothing more than a damp E-cloth and water. If he's happier with a spray, Lithofin Easy-Clean Spray (around £9.00/$14.58 from hardware stores) not only smells much nicer than meths, but won't risk setting the house on fire. Its highly active components dissolve dirt, oil and grease, and the stain-repellent additives will keep the surface looking cleaner for longer. Specially formulated for easy, streak-free cleaning of marble and limestone, it is also suitable for ceramics, glass and plastic surfaces.

My aluminium blinds are dirty and grimy and need a good clean. Help!

A good cream silver polish like HG Silver Shine Cream (http://www.hardware-ironmongers.com/details.aspx?code=2670600 around £5.00/$8.10) removes dirt upon application so you don't have to rub too hard when it comes to removing it. If the dirt isn't too ingrained, a wipe down with an HG Silver Shine Cloth would be easier (around £3.50/$5.67 https://www.lawsonshop.co.uk). Use a non-fluffy cloth to apply a small amount and rub it in gently. Leave to dry for about a minute, then polish off, regularly switching to a clean piece of cloth. When they're clean, dust regularly. Of all the venetian blind dusters on the market, the Touch To Clean microfibre glove (around £16.00/$25.92 a pair, from http://www.amazon.co.uk) is one of the best, both for speed and ease of use.

We have a navy blue, round stud rubber floor. Now there's a white stain from a damp towel left

overnight. We need to restore the colour? Help!

Rubber flooring can take just about anything thrown at it, except, as you've discovered, prolonged contact with water. Never leave anything damp lying around on it for any length of time, or a residue such as yours will accrue on the surface of the rubber. To get rid of it, you'll have to clean the whole surface with a floor stripper specially formulated for rubber floors, and then polish it up. The Rubber Flooring Company sells a floor care kit that contains both the stripper and the polish (in matt or gloss finish), as well as a day-to-day cleaner (http://www.therubberflooringcompany.co.uk/ around £23.00/$37.26).

Rubber is an environmentally friendly flooring and generally easy to keep clean. For general cleaning, never use abrasives or solvent cleaners, but instead apply a gentle one such as Ecover all-purpose cleaner (around £2.50/$4.05 from supermarkets). Dissolve one capful in half a bucket of warm water and clean the floor using a special rubber floor squeegee (from hardware stores, or around £4.00/$6.48 https://www.bargaintools.co.uk) which moulds to uneven floor surfaces, so leaving them dry.

I have cement water on two of my conservatory windows. I've tried scraping but it's not working. Help!

If the glass is smooth and not mottled, try using a glass window scraper (around £1.50/$2.43 from hardware stores). You don't need to wet the glass first, just scrape over the affected area. If that doesn't work, or if the glass is mottled, HG Extra Cement Grout Film Remover (hardware stores or around £10.50/$17.01 http://www.diytools.co.uk) will do the job. Dilute one part to 10 parts water and spread liberally over the stain. Leave for 15-20 minutes, but don't let it dry out – if it looks like drying out, apply more liquid – then scrub off with a scouring pad. Rinse well two or three times with water. If any white stains remain, repeat. Remove splashes on paint immediately. If you can't get hold of the HG remover, Lithofin Easy Care Cleaner (hardware stores or around £11.00/$17.82 (http://www.thenaturaltilestudio.com) might work. Add a squirt (20g) to a bucket of lukewarm water and apply to the surface. Wipe off using a clean cloth or mop, but no water. If any streaks remain, wipe them off using lukewarm water.

How do I clean my oven with an oven cleaner that's non-caustic. Help!

Bicarbonate of Soda is a good choice. Sprinkle over the oven interior and dampen with a water spray bottle. Leave it for 30 minutes to an hour and then wipe off. If burnt-in stains still aren't coming off leave it for longer, making sure it doesn't dry out. If it does dry, respray and leave for longer. Another great non-toxic option for ovens is the Magic Eraser Block £3.89/$6.30 from (http://www.lakeland.co.uk) or the Zam sponge eraser, £1.00/$1.62 from Poundland.

This is the quickest way to keep an oven clean, dampen and wipe and the grease is very quickly absorbed into the sponge. Wear rubber gloves or it will get all over your hands as well. Or try an all-purpose citrus-based cream cleaner such as Astonish Oven & Cookware Cleaner (£1.50/$2.43 http://www.partridgeshadleigh.co.uk). The Peta-approved Orange Mate Concentrate by Earth Friendly is also good for tackling really grimy surfaces (around £4.00/$6.48 http://www.ethicalsuperstore.com).

Washing in the dishwasher has made our wine glasses go cloudy. Can we make them clear again? Help!

Half-submerge one glass in a bowl of white vinegar for 10 minutes. Rinse, dry with a soft, lint-free cloth and hold up to the light: if you can't see a difference, the glass is 'etched', which is irreversible; if you can, it's salvageable. Soak the glass in warm vinegar for two hours, rinse and dry. If any cloudiness remains, dip some fine-grade steel wool in warm vinegar and gently rub. The cause could be the glasses rubbing against each other in the wash, too much detergent, too little rinse aid or too low a temperature. Wash any valuable glasses by hand, or use a dishwasher glass rack that keeps them separate. Before you run a wash, put a cup of vinegar on the lowest shelf, run for 10 minutes, stop the cycle, add detergent (not too much) and restart.

The panel on my stainless steel cooker is scratched. Is there a product that will get them out? Help!

They'll probably come off with T-Cut, a fine abrasive paste (around £6.00/$9.72 from hardware stores). Apply with a soft cloth in a circular motion, wipe off and buff – for an even result, you'll probably have to polish the whole panel. For more serious problems, (http://www.ulti-met.co.uk) provides an on-site service to remove scratches and blemishes from stainless steel. It also sells a stainless steel scratch removal and refinishing kit for around £60.00/$97.20. For a useful chart listing solutions to every kind of stainless steel cleaning problem, go to the British Stainless Steel Association's website, (http://www.bssa.org.uk).

I have a stain on my (light-coloured) Corian worktop, I think caused by fabric softener, and it won't shift. Help!

Corian surfaces are made from a blend of acrylic polymer and natural materials that are homogenous all the way through, so virtually any stain, burn or nick can be removed. Corian says it may be hard water staining, and recommends a limescale cleaner, such as Viakal or Limelite (around £2.50/$4.05 from supermarkets). Apply, leave for a few minutes, then wipe with a cloth in a circular motion. Wet a second cloth in hot, soapy water, wipe over and dry with a clean cloth. If that doesn't work, try Barkeepers Friend, apply with a damp cloth in a circular motion, rinse with warm, soapy water, then dry with a clean cloth/ paper towel. You may find that cleaning a small area brings back the original lustre, so you may have to clean a larger area. If the stain still doesn't shift get in touch with Corian at (http://corian.co.uk).

I use a water and a fabric softener but my towels still come out scratchy. Help!

Are you using too much detergent? Less, rather than more, produces cleaner, softer results – and for extra softness add a scoop of baking powder to the detergent tray and half a cup of white vinegar to the rinse tray. For an extra boost, soak them in a solution of Soda Crystals and water for an hour first. Tumble-drying your towels isn't as eco-friendly as line drying, but it will fluff them up.

There's a bad smell coming from the drum in my washer-dryer. Help!

Check the drain hose hasn't been dislodged by clutter under your sink and that your u-bend is clean, then do a maintenance wash. Run the machine empty on the hot or boil setting, using bicarbonate of soda or Soda Crystals, Ariel tablets, a dishwasher cleaner, or Affresh Washing Machine Cleaner

(http://shop.ukwhitegoods.co.uk

around £8.00/$12.96).

If that doesn't work, it may be that the machine is incorrectly installed. If you see it slowly filling when it's switched off, you'll need to call a plumber.

I have some new seagrass baskets that I use to store toys but they smell horrible. I need an effective and child-safe way of cleaning them that will remove the smell. Help!

Sprinkle all surfaces with bicarbonate of soda, place a bowl of vinegar inside, leave in a warm spot for a few days, then wipe off. For more power, use ammonia instead of vinegar but follow safety instructions, keep well away from your child until the process is complete and you've aired the boxes thoroughly after exposure to ammonia. If the smell persists, seal it in with a clear polyurethane wood varnish like Cuprinol Trade Polyurethane Varnish (around £12.00/$19.44 from hardware stores).

I've got red wine on my cream sofa. I've tried salt but it didn't work. Help!

Don't use hot water or soap – they set wine stains. Try soda water. If that doesn't work, milk is good on wine stains, ink, newsprint and red juice stains, but may well leave a smelly milk stain that will need shampooing. Alternatively, Wine Away is water-based, biodegradable and made from natural ingredients so safe around pets and children. It will remove red wine, cranberry juice, blood and other red stains from carpets and fabrics (around £11.00/$17.82 http://www.lakeland.co.uk).

Our toddler has scribbled all over our dark brown leather sofa with a biro. I tried cleaning the marks off with a sponge and washing-up liquid but it didn't work. Help!

Ethanol, or isopropyl (rubbing) alcohol, will remove ink stains from leather – even old, worn-in marks. It's found in all sorts of products you may already have: hairspray, medical wipes and stain removers such as Ecover Stain Remover (around £3.00/$4.86 from supermarkets). Milk also removes ink from all kinds of fabrics and surfaces. Be sure to test all of these on a hidden seam of your sofa first, especially the hairspray, which contains chemicals that might damage the leather. You can get pure ethanol from a pharmacy. Apply to a clean white cloth and dab gently on to the stain.

I've got water stains on my pine chest of drawers. Furniture sprays aren't removing them. Help!

Rubbing with mayonnaise, cigarette ash or toothpaste are the most popular tips for removing water marks from wood. I haven't tried cigarette ash. Mayonnaise seems to leave only a sticky mess, but toothpaste can do the trick. With a clean, damp cloth, gently rub white, non-gel toothpaste over the stain in a circular motion. Keep working at it for five minutes or so. As the mark fades, start to rub in the direction of the grain of the wood. Wash down with a damp cloth (be careful not to soak the wood) and apply a rich, nourishing wax such as Lord Sheraton Pure Beeswax Balsam (around £3.00/$4.86 from supermarkets) or Briwax Natural Creamed Beeswax (around £7.00/$11.34 from hardware stores). Apply with a soft cloth to small areas at a time and polish off before the wax dries. Don't use toothpaste on pine veneer which is easily damaged by too much rubbing. It can also lighten some woods. If this does happen, Briwax and Lord Sheraton make darkening waxes, or work a little brown shoe polish into the wood in the direction of the grain, wipe down and wax. Heat can also lift water stains out. Ironing over a towel is one way but you take the risk of damaging the wood if the iron is too hot and so isn't recommended. Place a hot water bottle over the stain and leave it there until it cools.

We've just taken up the decking from the patio of our new house. We're left with wood paint stains that have splashed down from the decking. Help!

You could try the Canadian-developed RemovAll system. This is a water-based paint-stripper and general coating remover that contains no nasty chemicals, is virtually odourless, 100% biodegradable, easy to use and won't burn your skin. There are 11 different formulations that are strong enough to remove epoxies, polyurethanes, powder coatings, gloss, emulsion and even graffiti. The type you need is RemovAll 320, which is designed to remove paint from porous surfaces such as brick, stone, concrete and wood (around £28.00/$45.36 for four litres, from (http://www.cirrus-systems.co.uk).

The suede sofas in our rented flat are covered with food dirt and general wear and tear. I don't want to have to pay for professional cleaning. Help!

Vacuum thoroughly, wipe with a dry towel, then try rubbing out any remaining marks. An ordinary white pencil rubber may work, but a suede rubber would be better. These are two-sided rubbers with a smooth side for cleaning and a rough surface for removing greasy and stubborn stains. You can get them from larger shoe shops ofor around £5.0/$8.10. Finish off by gently brushing with a suede brush. Cleaning the sofa yourself is risky. Look for the care label to see if you can use a wet cleaner, a solvent cleaner or both; it's important to use only specialist cleaners for suede or nubuck. Use a soft brush to loosen the dirt on more heavily soiled areas before you apply. Always pre-test on a hidden area and never allow the cleaner to dry on the surface, which could leave spot marks. Nubuck Foam Cleaner (around £12.00/$19.44) is a solvent-free foam, while Nubuck Protection (around £14.00/$22.68) helps guard against food and drink stains and will make future cleaning easier (http://www.springvaleleather.co.uk).

Vacuum regularly and don't position the sofa in direct sunlight, which can cause permanent fading.

Green chicken curry has turned our silver cutlery black. What did this, and can we clean them? Help!

It's the sulphur in the curry paste. Mayonnaise, mustard, vinegar and eggs have a similar effect. Wash the cutlery by hand, then clean with Goddard's Silver Dip (from hardware stores), which simply and safely removes tarnish from cutlery, jewellery and other small items. It works by chemically releasing sulphur from the surface of the silver, resulting in a bright, metallic finish. The silver itself is not affected and, after rinsing and drying, can be used again immediately. Be careful not to get the liquid on any non-silver surfaces or knife blades. Don't store silver in plastic bags or bags secured with elastic bands. Rubber also contains sulphur, so don't wear rubber gloves for cleaning or leave silver lying on rubber matting. Silver that's in regular use will keep its sheen far longer than if it's stored away in a drawer or cupboard.

We've had the builders in and dust has got into a large double-glazed window. It looks terrible. Do I have to replace it with a new unit? It was really expensive. Help!

Disassembling the unit is not a cost-efficient option. The Glass and Glazing Federation (http://www.ggf.org.uk/) thinks it is extremely unlikely that household dust or any other foreign body has entered the sealed unit. It suggests the dust is a desiccant – invisible under normal circumstances – which was placed in the spacer bar of the unit during manufacture to absorb moisture. Get the original installer of the window to inspect the damage and suggest a solution. The GGF is able to provide an expert witness service should an independent surveyor be required. In the unlikely event that it does turn out to be building dust, you might have a case for an insurance claim. Is accidental damage included in your cover? Did your insurer know you were having the work done? Always tell your insurance company when you have builders in, especially if you have any burglar-friendly scaffolding erected. If you don't, your insurance may be invalidated.

I've got bird droppings on my car. They've been there a while and have dried up. Can I get rid of them without damaging the paintwork? Help!

What you need is Bird S*!t Remover (around £8.00/$12.96   http://www.birdshitremover.co.uk). Designed to remove bird droppings from boats and boat covers, it will not, according to the manufacturer, damage fibreglass, wood, waterproofed boat covers or any other material, and can be used on cars, including soft-tops. If the droppings have been left to dry in, especially in hot weather, the acidic lime in them may have penetrated and damaged the car's paintwork. Bodywork repair shops and some of the more comprehensive car valeting services, such as Essex-based Clean Image, offer a paint correction service called wet sanding (from around £30.00/$48.40 http://www.clean-image.co.uk).

This will greatly reduce, and can completely remove, small, localised stains caused by bird droppings, scuffs, key scratches and chemical burns, or just bring dull and faded paintwork back to life.

The rings on my electric cooker have gone rusty and have lots of burnt-in marks on them. I'm scared of scrubbing too hard or using abrasives. Help!

If your cooker isn't ancient and you still have the handbook, check to see if any specific cleaning products are recommended. If you've lost it you may find it's available to view online. Tricity Bendix and Zanussi recommend Homecare 4 Hob Electric Hotplate Polish

(arnd £5.00/$8.10
http://www.appliancespares2go.com)
to restore, blacken and protect rings, while Creda and Hotpoint favour Easy-Do Hobcare Sealed Hot Plate Restorer (around £4.50 http://www.buyspares.co.uk).

I used to clean the red tiles on my windowsill with Cardinal red tile polish but I can't find it any more. Help!

Try Tableau Red Tile Polish, a rich wax polish often advertised as an ideal substitute for Cardinal. Or Tableau Black Tile Polish, which its makers say restores colour and lustre to black unsealed concrete or cement-based steps, floors and unsealed black wood surfaces

(around £8.00/$12.96 http://www.heritage-homeandgarden.co.uk).

Water got into our wooden kitchen cabinets from a washing machine leak. Now the cupboards smell damp and musty nothing will get rid of the smell. It seems to be spreading as well. Help!

Cover all the interior surfaces of your cupboards with a thick paste of bicarbonate of soda or borax and water. Smear kitchen towels with the paste, then stick against the sides and top, leaving a small border for the tape to stick to. Leave for two hours and scrub off with warm water. Leave the doors open until the wood is dry, then place a bowl of activated charcoal in each cupboard – try Eheim Ehfikarbon, around £4.00/$6.48 from aquarium shops.

We get a lot of traffic pollution in our house from the busy main road outside. We need to freshen the air. Help!

There are a vast number of makes and models of air purifiers on the market. Factors to consider before buying include initial outlay versus running and filter replacement costs, noise levels and health issues. Ozone purifiers are sometimes marketed as whole-house systems, but their main function is to clear heavily polluted, unoccupied areas damaged by fire or flood. Ozone has been known to cause respiratory problems and these purifiers are considered by some to be a health risk, as are ionizer purifiers, even though they generate only low doses of ozone. Systems that use the HEPA (high-efficiency particulate air) filter are the most widely recommended by medical professionals. Look for those that carry the British Allergy Foundation's seal of approval and beware of 'HEPA-type' filters. 'The new generation of silent, non-ionizing air-filtration systems are also very effective – though expensive to buy, they are cheap to run and there are no filters to change. Try the Airfree system (from around £164.00 /$265.71 http://www.airsterilisers.co.uk).

Our stainless steel cutlery is dishwasher-safe but it now has a slight 'bluey' finish, like tempered steel. We've tried special polishes. Help!

Either the cutlery hasn't been rinsed properly over a period of time or it's been in contact with hot fat or acidity. Too much detergent in the dishwasher, especially lemon-based concentrates, may also be the cause. That said, such stains should come off easily with baking soda or a good stainless-steel cleaner such as Barkeepers Friend (widely available). Sheffield cutlery experts W Wright Cutlery & Silverware say that ingrained staining on stainless steel is a rare phenomenon. In most cases, it's due to something that's become deposited on the steel, rather than to any attack on the steel itself. The most common cause is attack by one of the proprietary dip solutions used for removing tarnish from silver. Although excellent for silver and silver-plate, these solutions should never be allowed to come into contact with stainless steel. They contain acids that etch the steel, first giving it an iridescent rainbow stain and then ultimately etching it to a dull grey. W Wright recommend a more vigorous stainless-steel cleaner, Solvol's Autosol (around £4.00/$6.48 from hardware stores).

My front path is made of red and white Edwardian tiles that desperately need a clean. I've tried scrubbing them but the dirt is very ingrained. I don't want to lose any of the colour and don't know what to use. Help!

Lithofin KF Tile Restorer is an alkaline, solvent-free cleansing concentrate suitable for all coloured antique ceramic tiles, glazed or unglazed (around £15.00/$24.30 from tile shops). After giving the path a thorough sweeping, test on a small area, then apply neat or diluted in water at a ratio of up to 1:10, depending on the degree of soiling. The Tile Doctor recommends its Remove & Go for old tiles

(around £17.00/$27.54 http://www.tiledoctor.co.uk).

A non-flammable, multipurpose stripper, it's formulated with a long dwell-time to remove most ingrained stains from ceramic tiles. With a scrubbing brush or sponge, apply a small amount of remover to no more than 2m sq (22ft sq) at a time. Leave to stand until the residue softens – about an hour, but keep checking because it mustn't dry out. Agitate with a scrubbing brush or plastic scourer, then wipe up with a clean, absorbent white cotton towel or sponge.

The coarse cord carpet in my daughter's rented home needs a good clean. There are several dark spots that won't come out. What should she do? Help!

First, she should check her tenancy documents. Many stipulate that carpets and curtains be professionally cleaned when the tenancy ends. Otherwise, stubborn stains can sometimes be removed with oxygen bleach (Wizz Oxi Ultra Plus, around £23.00/$37.26 from supermarkets). It's non-toxic and, at its normal dissolve ratio, can be used safely with colours. Mix a teaspoon with 500ml warm water. When the granules have dissolved, dab with a sponge or soft cloth. Leave to dry. If the mark is still there, make a paste with two scoops of bleach and one of warm water. Colour test by applying a small spot to a hidden bit of carpet first; leave for 30 minutes, then dab off with warm water. If, when the spot has dried, the colour has held, apply to the stain. If not, don't. If this were your own carpet, you may want to go ahead, preferring a slightly lighter mark to the stain itself.

Why does every loo brush I use turn bright orange soon after I've bought it? I've tried all sorts of cleaners and bleaches but nothing stops it. Help!

Iron in the water supply causes brown, pink or orange stains. This will be exacerbated if you use chlorine bleach which will react with the iron. Try soaking the brush in lemon juice or vinegar. If this isn't enough, use a biodegradable limescale remover such as Ecover Limescale Remover (around £3.50/$5.67 from supermarkets), and clean your toilets with a biodegradable citric acid-based cleaner such as Bio-D (around £2.00/$3.24 http://www.honestycosmetics.co.uk). Descaler rings are chemical-free magnetic rings that you drop into the cistern. Lasting up to five years, they polarise the calcium and prevent stains and limescale build-up (around £15.00/$24.30 http://www.ecozone.com).

A tom cat has sprayed all over my mahogany dining table. Help!

HG Meubeline Furniture Restorer removes stains, haze and water marks, and disguises scratches, on varnished, oiled, waxed or untreated furniture. It comes in dark or light wood versions (around £8.00/$12.96 http://www.amazon.co.uk). Liberon Ring Remover is a non-colouring remover of water and heat marks from highly polished surfaces (around £7.50/$12.15 http://www.diytools.co.uk).

The glass doors on our wood-burning stove are covered in a heavy, tarry deposit which makes it almost impossible to see the fire inside. Even with a lot of hard scraping, it's very difficult to remove. Help!

Hotspot Glass Cleaner dissolves smoke stains and tar/creosote deposits from wood, coal or oil-burning stoves (around £5.00/$8.10 on e-bay.co.uk). It's extremely flammable, so make sure the glass is cool. It will not damage paint or enamel, but cover any carpet surround. Don't inhale it and protect your hands before applying. Leave the foam for five minutes before wiping off with a damp cloth, rubbing gently; use a nylon scouring pad on stubborn stains. It's probably worth having your flues checked to make sure everything's working as it should. For less aggressive stains and regular cleaning, Astonish Multi-Purpose Orange Cleaning Paste with orange oil (around £1.35/$2.18 http://www.partridgeshadleigh.co.uk) is a biodegradable multipurpose cleaner that removes tough stains from glass, ceramic hobs, ovens, stovetops, pans, cookware, baths, tiles, sinks, chrome, metals, uPVC windows, doors and patio furniture, and leaves a lovely orange-fresh aroma.

The sealant on our UPVC windows is starting to go black, especially in the corners. I've tried cleaning them without getting anywhere. Help!

Assuming you've tried vinegar, which can remove lighter stains, dilute two parts warm water to one part chlorine bleach. Apply to the stain, leave for 15 minutes, then rinse well. If – and only if – the stain appears lighter, repeat until it has gone. You might have to keep at it over days, even weeks. For faster results try proprietary sprays such as Astonish Mould & Mildew Remover (around £1.50/$2.43 from supermarkets) or HG Hagesan Mould Spray (around £5.00/$8.10 http://www.homecareessentials.co.uk), but again don't give up too soon and be prepared to reapply if necessary. Wear rubber gloves, follow manufacturers' instructions and rinse thoroughly each time, especially between applications of bleach and any other product. If all else fails, get a handyman to cut out the marks and reseal.

We were flooded last year. The brick step leading

to our conservatory and the terracotta tiles inside have dried out but now there's a white deposit there. It looks like paint. I can't do anything to make it look better – scrubbing makes it worse. Help!

The mineral salts inside the terracotta have come to the surface. It sounds as if you will have to strip the floor of its sealer and reapply, but before going down this route, try a specialised tile stain remover. Aqua Mix NanoScrub is an abrasive cream cleaner designed to work where other cleaners won't. It utilises NanoSTTM (nano-sized particles) to penetrate below tough stains, dissolve and lift them out. Especially effective for cleaning rough or textured surfaces. Also removes factory applied waxes and floor finishes, light grout residue (including epoxy), rubber and pencil marks, light mineral deposits, ground-in dirt and most sealer residues. It's non-toxic, non-flammable and non-acidic (around £13.00/$21.06 from tile shops). Or try Aqua Mix Phosphoric Acid Cleaner (around £10.00/$16.19 from tile shops) which removes mineral deposits, rust stains and efflorescence. Handle with care and test on a small, hidden area first. To strip the sealer, mix one part Pro-Clean tile and grout cleaner (around £12.00/$19.44 from tile shops) with three parts warm water; apply using a scrubbing brush or buffing machine. Don't kneel in it and avoid contact with your skin. Leave for five to 10 minutes, but don't let it dry out on the surface. Mop up the dirty solution and rinse thoroughly with clean water. When the tiles are bone dry, apply a sealer, such as Seal & Go (around £16.00/$25.92) – terracotta tiles are so porous, they will need eight or nine coats. The problem with efflorescence such as this is that it will recur, but not to such a great degree. Keep it at bay by cleaning frequently with a pH-neutral cleaner, such as Neutral Tile Cleaner (around £11.00/$16.20) or Aqua Mix Concentrated Tile Cleaner (around £9.00/$14.58).

Online tileshop: http://www.tiledoctor.co.uk; online grout protection: http://www.groutprotection.co.uk/.

My washing machine is 18 months old. Most of my dark and black clothes come out with little bits of white fibres on them, at least I think they're fibres. I brush them off as best I can before ironing but they never really come off. Help!

Instead of brushing off the lint, put the affected clothes in the tumble dryer for 10 to 15 minutes and the fluff will magically disappear. If you overload the washing machine, the fabrics will agitate against each other and there won't be enough space for a proper rinse cycle. This problem can also occur if you wash dark fabrics with lighter-coloured towels, knits or other soft-piled items, or if you don't empty those bits of fluff from pockets before laundering. Worse, if a tissue gets forgotten, it can leave residue that can last for several wash cycles. Reduce the risk of this by turning all pockets inside out and rinsing off any fluff under the tap. Don't overload your machine, and try turning dark clothing inside out before laundering. Regularly check the fluff traps on your washer, usually located behind a removable flap near the base of the front of the machine.

My water is a blue/greeny colour. Is this, as I've been told, copper? Is it harmful? Help!

The Environment Agency's Drinking Water

Inspectorate advises that if your water looks cloudy or discoloured, tastes different or smells funny, then you should contact your water company immediately. Check with your neighbours to see if they have the same problem. Put two samples in clean glass jars, seal them and keep them to show the water company and, if it is involved later, the inspectorate. Make a note of the date and time, the appearance and any problems you have had. If the water company gives no satisfactory explanation, contact the Consumer Council for Water (http://www.ccwater.org.uk). The erosion of pipes in your plumbing system can create unacceptable copper levels in drinking water, which could be a health risk, especially to babies and sufferers of some disorders. Warning signs are a metallic taste, usually detectable before the levels are high enough to cause concern, and blue/green or blue stains around pipes and sinks. Algae turns water blue/green. Dangerously high levels will have been detected by your water company, but if you have a private water supply, a well or borehole, it should be investigated immediately. If your drinking water is not supplied by a water company, contact the environmental health department of your local council. A leaflet providing further information for owners and users of private water supplies is available at (http://dwi.defra.gov.uk).

I have stains on my polished slate. Help!

HG Super Remover (around £8.00/$12.96 from tile shops) is a strong cleaner for tiled and stone floors. Dilute one part to 10 parts water. Apply with a brush or mop, then thoroughly scrub. Leave for a few minutes; scrub again. Wash off with a cloth, frequently rinsing and wringing it out, then rinse twice using clean water. If any stain remains, repeat using one part cleaner to four parts water. Or try Fila Stone Stain Remover (around £17.00/$27.54). Dilute 1:5, pour on, leave for one minute, scour, wash and rinse. If stain remains, repeat with a dilution of 1:2. If all else fails, Lithofin Stain-Away (around £20.00/$32.40) is a powerful alkaline solution that will remove stains from ceramic and stone. It's ineffective when mixed with water (so make sure slate is bone dry first) and contains dichloromethane, wear a mask and avoid contact with skin and eyes.

I have some old bricks with bits of mortar on them. I want to get this off so that I can reuse them? Help!

If it's chunks of mortar then chiselling off is the only way. If it's just a film, an acid cleaner will help. Ever Build's high-strength Brick & Patio Cleaner (around £7.00/$11.34 from builder's merchants, hardware stores or e-bay), is a fast-acting cleaner that will dissolve mortar film, ingrained dirt and most paints from brick, stone and concrete. It's an extremely aggressive acid product, so test it first on an unseen area, wear protective gear, shield other surfaces and follow disposal guidelines. Pour into a plastic container and apply using a scrubbing brush or stiff bristle paintbrush, working well into the substrate. Leave for 20 minutes maximum, then scrub with cold water, repeating if necessary.

I've inherited an old Gladstone bag that needs complete restoration. Help!

Try your local Yellow Pages or http://www.yell.com/

under Saddlers & Harness Makers, some of whom will offer repair services for all sorts of leather goods as well as for saddles. For example, Martin Ashworth, of The Leather Workshop Antique Restoration & Repairs in Anglesey (http://www.mlworkshop.co.uk) is a bespoke saddle manufacturer who has diversified into repairing and replicating all sorts of antique leather items – chairs, coats, even footballs – and has experience of Gladstone bag restoration. He'd need to see yours before he could give you a quote, but a couple of photographs would suffice. To give you an idea of cost, a complete restoration, which would include dismantling the bag, recolouring and reconditioning the leather, hand-stitching to preserve the original stitching holes, waxing and polishing the finished repairs, plus hand-making a new handle if required, would be in the region of £450/$729 – £500/$810. If you couriered the bag to him for inspection, he would contact you before any work took place to discuss the best way forward.

I have inherited a 1930s glazed porcelain vase that reeks of stale tobacco. It's a Moorcroft vase and we're nervous about what we can use to get rid of it, we've tried rinsing in washing up liquid without success. Help!

Moorcroft Potteries said the smell of smoke shouldn't linger, so this may mean that your vase has crazed (developed tiny cracks). Washing the vase is not advisable because the clay could absorb the water and eventually crack. Don't do anything else at this stage until more is known. To track down a local expert, the Conservation Register has a database of accredited conservator-restorers in the UK and Ireland (http://www.conservationregister.com/index.asp).

The non-slip floor of our shower cubicle has become greasy. It has a slightly rough surface and feels like Velcro when I wipe it. I've tried lemon juice but it didn't work. Help!

Try drenching a cloth or sheets of kitchen towel in lemon juice or vinegar. Place over the surface, weigh down with something heavy and leave overnight. Slipsolve's Safe Kleen has been specially formulated to clean Safe Grip's anti-slip bathroom surfaces, but its manufacturers say that it will work on any surface and can also be used as a multipurpose cleaner

(around £12.50/$20.25

http://www.slipsolve.com/shop.html).

To remove grease from the shower tray, apply liberally to the surface with a sponge and allow a few minutes' contact time. Rinse thoroughly and dry. Stubborn stains may require more than one treatment. For general cleaning, use two capfuls in a bucket of water for light duty, four for heavy duty.

We had some boxes stacked indoors but against an outside wall. When we moved them we discovered mould all over the wall and carpet. The area is badly ventilated. We've cleaned and painted but can't get the mould out of the carpet. It's also appearing around the upstairs windows. Help!

There are three types of damp: condensation, penetrating and rising. Rising damp would affect only the ground floor. Your damp is coming from an outside wall, so it may be penetrating damp caused by a problem with a leaky roof, pipe or guttering, and these should be checked. Inefficient loft and cavity wall insulation would also contribute to the ventilation problem. Oxygen bleach is non-toxic, environmentally-friendly and colour-safe, can be used on many types of carpet, fabric and upholstery. Unlike chlorine bleach it's compatible with other household cleaners. Always test on a hidden area first, though, especially if the carpet has wool content. You can buy 100% pure oxygen bleach (chemical name sodium percarbonate from (http://mistralie.co.uk) for around £7.00/$11.34 kg. Mix the powder with water to make a paste, apply to the stain and leave for several hours. Mould spores are a health hazard, so you must wear gloves and a mask. It mustn't dry out, so check it regularly and moisten with a damp cloth or extra paste if necessary. Rinse off by dabbing with a damp cloth or kitchen towel – never rub carpet stains or you could permanently damage the fibre. Supermarkets and hardware stores sell Oxygen bleach products like Wizz and Oxi Clean but they won't make such a smooth paste. If the carpet has a high wool content or the test wasn't successful, the National Carpet Cleaners Association suggests diluting one quarter of a teaspoon only of carpet shampoo and one egg cup of vinegar in two litres of tepid water. Blot over the stain, cover with five or six layers of kitchen roll, put a phone directory on top and leave for 24 hours. This will absorb stains at the base of the fibres. If that doesn't work, call in a professional. If you don't find out the cause of the mould, it will return.

Our 1870s hall has a beautiful cornice of thistles and roses. I've been cleaning it with a bamboo skewer which does work but is so slow. There must be a quicker way. Help!

The Peel Away 1 Paint Removal System is especially suited to removing multi-layers of paint from carved or moulded surfaces and it usually takes only one application. Wearing protective gloves, mask and clothing, spread the ready-mixed paste over the cornice, making sure every detail is covered. Then lay the special laminated tissue cover over the paste and leave until all the paint is emulsified. Give it 24 hours to dry, then peel off. Peel Away 1 works on softwood, bricks, concrete and plaster, including plain or enriched cornices and ornate ceiling roses, metals and fibreglass. It comes in packs of 3kg (around £23.00/$37.26) or 12kg (around £64.00/$103.68), including instructions, application tool and sufficient covers, from (http://www.decoratingdirect.co.uk) – 12kg should cover around 3.2 square metres at the maximum 3mm thickness. Neutralising the surface afterwards is an essential part of the treatment, too – the 3kg pack comes with a neutraliser, the 12kg one does not. Or neutralise with white vinegar. Cornices of stone or marble must be protected against colour damage by using the more costly Peel Away 7 (around £100.00/162.01 kg) – this is less aggressive and there's no need to neutralise, but a final swab with methylated spirits is recommended.

We've got black marker pen on our wooden table. We've tried soap and water without success. Now we're being advised to strip, varnish, sand, stain, revarnish. There must be a cheaper way. Help!

You could try contacting the marker pen manufacturer, who should be able to tell you what your chances are. They may even be able to recommend a solvent that won't damage your table. Some graffiti can be rubbed out with a pencil eraser, others with ordinary white non-gel toothpaste – don't use a whitening or baking soda brand, which may bleach the wood, and test on a hidden surface area first. The following can work, too, but do test it first: wet ink is easier to remove than dry, so go over the mark with fresh pen, then wipe the ink off before it dries. Alternatively, Graffiti Go! (around £9.00/$14.58 http://www.decoratingdirect.co.uk) works safely on a variety of surfaces, including wood, removing marker pen, paint, leather dye, crayon and chewing gum. It's solvent-free, pH neutral and cleans off with water.

My old down quilt/duvet has leaky seams and is losing its feathers. I used to know a place that cleaned the down filling and recovered but not any more. I don't want to throw it away. Help!

The Feather Company offers a full pillow and duvet re-covering service. (http://www.thefeathercompany.com) It can also turn your existing feather- and down-filled items into something new, make duvets from old pillows, eiderdowns and cushions, re-stuff sofa cushions and make made-to-measure feather- and down-filled duvets, pillows and cushions of all shapes and sizes, working to your own templates and measurements, if desired. Send them your duvet and they'll call to confirm the cost before proceeding with any work. Once approved, they'll remove the filling, fluff it up in a chamber and add extra feathers if required. Re-covering prices range from around £40.00/$64.80 for a single duvet to £60.00/$97.20 for a double, £70.00/$113.40 for king size and

£80.00/$129.60 for super king size.

I've got a mark from my denim jeans on our light patterned (non-vinyl) wallpaper. I've tried rubbing it out with an eraser but it didn't work and roughed up the surface. Help!

If a soft pencil eraser roughs up the surface, it sounds as if it will be very difficult to remove the dye without doing more damage to the wallpaper. The following might work but must be tested on an inconspicuous part of the wall first. Cover the stain with a paste made of bicarbonate of soda (baking powder) and water; leave for five to 10 minutes, but don't let it dry out. Gently dab off with a damp cloth. Baking powder can have a bleaching effect, so don't even attempt this on dark wallpapers. JML Magic Eraser (around £5.00/$8.10 http://www.robertdyas.co.uk) and Poundland's Zam Magic Eraser Block (£1.00/$1.62)) are soft, non-abrasive cleaning sponges which shift all sorts of stubborn stains from a wide variety of surfaces. They come in a block which you cut to size and dampen before gently rubbing over the stain. They can be used on walls and floors, on wood and vinyl, for burnt-on food on hobs and pans, and tea and coffee stains on cups and mugs. Don't use them on any varnished, polished or dark surfaces.

Our hall floor is covered in Marmoleum. The specialist cleaner used to come in two separate bottles, making it a two-step process which left the marmoleum shining clean. Now it's sold as a single product and we can't get the same lovely finish. Help!

You can use other products but avoid harsh alkalis,

those with high pH content, such as ammonia, chemical vinyl floor cleaners and wax furniture polish. But it may be that you're not giving the new product a chance. For the original lustre finish you're after, several correctly applied applications of the manufacturer's recommended product, Monel, is your best bet because it leaves a protective film that restores the original appearance after each clean. (£6.30/$10.20 http://www.completelyflooring.co.uk). If your flooring hasn't been treated regularly, it may need several treatments with Monel to bring back the as new look. Incorrect application, especially wrong dilution ratios, could also have caused the problem. To keep your floor looking at its best, mop up spills as soon as possible to prevent spots becoming stains; rinse and allow to dry thoroughly before applying polish; use a clean mop head; clean on a regular basis; use doormats, plus protectors for sharp furniture legs. Don't use too much water or apply finish to a floor with surface dirt, and remember two or three thin coats are better than one thick one.

I've got greasy hand and hair marks on my leather chairs. Help!

For light grease marks dissolve one part washing-up liquid in five parts lukewarm water. Dab with the solution, don't over-wet, leave for a few minutes and wipe off. Always test for colourfastness on a hidden area of the chair first and use a weaker solution if necessary. As the hair marks have probably been worn in over time, a leather furniture degreaser may be the only answer for these. Leather Degreaser

(around £15.00/$24.30

http://www.furnitureclinic.co.uk) is a thick paste that draws out oil and grease stains from all types of leather except suede and nubuck. It's recommended for head grease marks, patches on the armrests, cooking oil, air freshener and food spills. Clean the leather first with a damp cloth dipped in a little Glycerine soap. Apply the paste with a paintbrush and leave for about 30 minutes. Once it's completely dry, vacuum off the powder. Repeat if necessary. Be aware, however, that once the grease has been removed, the leather may need recolouring. If you do have to recolour, Furniture Clinic has an enormous database of shades and can match virtually any one you want. Its kits are designed for public use and it provides full instructions, including where to cut a sample piece to send for colour matching if necessary.

Our 70s teak G-plan Nathan furniture has been sun-bleached and marked. Can we restore it to its original condition and colour? Help!

Clarkes Furnishers, of Maidstone (http://www.clarkesfurnishers.co.uk) stocks and restores a large range of second-hand Ercol and Nathan furniture. Chris Clarke, its MD, says, 'Anybody who is handy at DIY and does their own decorating should be able to tackle this job. First, remove the old lacquer with paint stripper and scraper, then neutralise the wood with methylated spirits and coarse/medium steel wool. This will also remove any remaining wax. Then, using 240 production paper, fine-sand along the grain to remove residual marks and scratches. If badly faded, some stain may be needed to restore the colour. Reseal the surface with clear lacquer, if sprayed, or polyurethane semi-matt, if brushed on. Finally, use very fine steel wool and wax along the grain to bring back the surface finish to match the rest of the item. Using masking tape helps to restrict spreading to areas not involved.' Pick up a tips and advice leaflet on how to prepare and stain wood from Homebase, or download from http://www.homebase.co.uk.

How do we clean our Chinese wool rugs? Can we do it at home? Can we clean just the tassles? Help!

Some Turkish and Indian woven rugs (ie, without pile) can be cleaned safely at home but Chinese and Persian rugs should always be left to the professionals. They'll test for colour-fastness, which can vary within the same rug, and for the pH of the rug's cleaning residues. Unfortunately, there's no safe quick fix for fringes either, and you may end up ruining the carpet if you tackle these yourself. Oriental carpet manufacturers Hill & Co Rugs (http://www.hillcorugs.com) will answer any queries and happily recommend a cleaner near you. The cost should be around £15.00/$24.30 a square metre. Its website carries an emergency stain spot removal guide for Oriental rugs, though they stress that it's best to call in the professionals wherever possible, and will not be responsible for damage incurred.

How do I clean my plastic shower curtain? I've spent hours scrubbing at the mould and scum without success. Help!

Most plastic, fabric and vinyl shower curtains can be laundered in the washing machine so check the care label. But don't wash plastic alone: shove in a few towels, too – these will rub up against the curtains and stop them getting mangled or crinkly. Powdered detergent is better than liquid. For a boost, add two tablespoons of bicarbonate of soda to the detergent tray. Select a delicates cycle, one you manually set to rinse; before rinsing, add a cup of white vinegar to the water and leave to soak for two hours. Don't tumble dry. Or soak in a mild vinegar solution in the bath (three cups for a half-filled tub). Vinegar and tea tree oil are great natural mould busters. Scrub stubborn stains with a paste of salt and vinegar. Make a preventative mist by mixing two teaspoons of tea tree oil and half a pint of water in a plant sprayer.

I got massage oil on my brand new duvet cover (cotton). I laundered it at a low temperature but the stain hasn't gone and spread when I ironed it. It's yellowish and about 15cm in diameter. Help!

Exposing stains to heat by ironing or tumble-drying is one of the big no-no's of stain removal. Oil stains quickly penetrate deep into the fibres, so now you've very probably set the stain permanently. If you hadn't ironed it, the cure would have been simple. Non-gel washing-up liquid is brilliant for oily stains. For grease and non-sugar tannin (black tea, coffee, neat, non-fermented alcohol), squirt both sides and rinse in hot water; use cold water for protein stains. The other two big stain removal 'don'ts' are: don't use hot water or heat on protein stains and don't use soap on tannin stains. You can tell a protein stain by its source: those resulting from the bodily functions of humans and animals are protein, as are those that come from the earth. Many basic food stains, such as egg, milk and cheese, come from animal products, so are classified as protein stains. Some food stains, such as gravy, chocolate and tomato sauce, are a protein/grease combination, and should be kept away from hot water. Most liquid stains, however, such as tea, coffee, alcohol, perfumes and inks, are tannin stains and should be treated as quickly as possible in the hottest water the fabric can take, avoiding soap at all costs. If you have no luck, check your insurance. Some accidental damage policies cover spills on to upholstery and carpets but exclude linen and clothing. A few, like Saga's Cover Plus include linen.

Why do clothes come out of our washing machine with brown spots? We replaced the machine but it still happens. Pre-soaking or stain removers don't make any difference. Now I'm scared to put some light-coloured fabrics in at all. What's causing it? How can we get rid of the spots? Help!

Since you have replaced your washing machine, a broken seal (which would let oil into the system) or metallic debris (such as part of a zip) caught in the door seal are unlikely culprits. Other possibilities are a build-up of fabric softener residue or wrong installation. Washing machines must never be laid on their side or oil can leak from the motor and infect washing. You've probably got iron in your water supply. It causes brown, pink or orange stains. This will be exacerbated if you use chlorine bleach, which will react with the iron. Copper in your water supply will leave green or grey stains. Descale your machine with Ultima washing machine descaler (around £2.00 from Waitrose) and avoid chlorine. If the problem persists, installing a water filter may be the only option, but first have the water analysed. Freepost a sample to Acorn Water in

Co Cork, Ireland (http://www.acornwater.com).

For around £76.00/$123.12 they'll make a report that you can download online. As to removing the stains, they may be permanent, but try washing in a combination of Ecover's non-biological detergent and Ecover chlorine-free natural oxygen bleach. As an added booster, apply neat liquid non-bio detergent to both sides of the stains, or use a paste of powder detergent mixed with a little water. Wash on the hottest cycle the fabric can take.

My feather-filled pillows need cleaning. Help!

Ducks and geese spend most of their time on water, and feather and down pillows are extremely washable. As you have lots of pillows, the idea of washing them at home probably doesn't appeal. But it's not so much the washing as the getting them dry and fluffy that is the problem. Take them to a launderette and dry them in one of those big dryers, with a few tennis balls (medium heat, not hot or they might melt) to pummel them. I don't dry-clean my clothes, because of the cost and the chemicals involved, and I would never dry-clean my bedding. The industry has started replacing the problem chemical perchloroethylene, known as 'perc' with other chemicals. Some cleaners now offer a service called GreenEarth. This uses the chemical siloxane, which isn't as nasty as perchloroethylene and carries none of those toxic, lingering odours, but still doesn't get the thumbs-up from Greenpeace. 'Because heat and chlorine are required to produce siloxanes, manufacture of these chemicals could lead to the formation of dioxin, a potent cancer-causing substance in humans,' it says. Greenpeace asks that we urge our dry cleaners to offer a non-toxic alternative. The most successful in terms of results is the CO2 method. This has yet to reach our high streets but is getting the thumbs-up in the US. Carbon dioxide is naturally abundant in our environment, and it can be collected as a byproduct of industrial processes such as alcohol production. It also has a deodorising effect, so your clothes and bedding come back smelling pleasant and fresh.

I bought a 1950s suede and leather chair on eBay. It's lovely but stinks of smoke. Baking soda and vinegar didn't work. It cost a fortune. Help!

Whatever is producing the odour must have penetrated the interior upholstery of your chair and footstool. Car valeting companies are the cigarette smoke specialists. A sophisticated system called Aromatek is the permanent solution, says the car valeting company Euroshine (http://www.euroshine.co.uk). Aromatek uses dry vapour produced from a blend of more than 32 essential oils designed chemically to neutralise and permanently remove odours such as those produced by 'tobacco smoke, animals, food and people'. The dry vapour penetrates deep into the porous surfaces inside the upholstery. It can also be used for smelly air conditioning systems. 'It can be expensive, depending on the time needed,' Euroshine admits, 'but so long as the treatment is done properly, the results are amazing. It takes between three and five hours.' To find the nearest valeting company offering this service, contact Autosmart (http://www.autosmart.co.uk).

I left a wet rubbish bag on our kitchen floor over

a whole weekend whilst I was away. Now the light beech vinyl floor has a big purple stain on it. I've tried bleach, detergent, steel wool without success. Help!

Dye stains are difficult, sometimes impossible, to remove. Ammonia might work (use as directed for isopropyl alcohol below), but on older types of lino and vinyl it will leave its own mark. Oven cleaner might do the trick on older lino, but will leave a bright pink mark on some types of newer vinyl. If you try either of these methods, test in an inconspicuous area first; behind the fridge, say. When having new flooring laid, it's always a good idea to keep some of the cuttings as test material for times such as this. Get some pure Isopropyl (rubbing) alcohol from a computer accessory shops, or online (around £10.00 http://www.maplin.co.uk). Again, always test before applying. If a direct application doesn't remove the stain, saturate a white cloth and leave it covering the stain, checking, wiping and reapplying as necessary. Isopropyl alcohol is flammable. Open the windows, remove all children and pets, wear gloves and a mask, and rinse off thoroughly.

Several of the glass panes of my sash windows have got scratches on them. Help!

Try running your fingernail over the scratches, if it does not get caught they can probably be polished out. Mix some Cerium Oxide with a little water and apply with a chamoix leather

(around £5.25/$8.50 http://www.homecrafts.co.uk). Or you could invest in a glass polishing kit from (http://www.glasspolishshop.co.uk), around £21.00/$34.02, which comes with full instructions and special drill attachment pads and polishers. They also sell a cerium oxide polishing compound (around £12.00/$19.44). If the scratches run deeper, you will have to call in a glazier. Scratchglass's prices for polishing range between around £60.00/$97.20 and £100/$162 per pane. You might find it more economical to replace the glass. To find a reputable firm in your area, TrustMark (http://www.trustmark.org.uk/) a recently-established award-winning scheme supported by consumer groups and the building industry, has a list of approved glaziers. It also registers builders, plumbers, electricians, painter and decorators, roofers, landscape gardeners and damp-proof specialists.

My black acrylic Magistretti coffee table has got scratches all over the surface. I want to disguise or, even better, remove them? Help!

Apply Brasso (around £2.50/$4.05 from supermarkets and hardware stores) with a soft, clean cloth in small circular strokes, much as you would if you were polishing a car. When it has dried into a powder, rub off with another clean cloth, pressing down firmly. You may have to do this several times. Brasso is currently enjoying a renaissance due to its remarkable plastic polishing properties – it will remove scratches from iPods, MP3 players, CDs, DVDs and other optical discs. Apply to the reflective surface of the disc, along the radius (in straight lines between the edge and centre). Alternatively, for your table use Xerapol Acrylic Scratch Remover, which you can get at car and motorbike accessory shops (around £7.00/$11.34). Clean the surface and apply a little paste. Using a soft, clean cotton cloth or cotton wool pad, polish the scratched areas using heavy pressure for two to three minutes. For deep scratches, repeat several times. Remove residue and polish up.

We have moved to a house with 1950s solid oak floors. They're in very good condition and we want to keep them that way. Help!

To keep your floors looking good, avoid exposing them to damaging scratches from grains of dirt and sand by placing a floor mat at the entrance to every room. Protect from furniture scratches by placing felt guards at contact points. Never wet-mop wooden floors – use either an E-cloth mop, a wrung-out mop or a dry mop and spray, which forms just enough moisture on the floor to clean it. If you have indoor plants, don't stand them on the floor, even in a tray. And beware of worn-down high heels, because these can pierce the wood. As for maintenance, Ruth Shann, of Real Oak Floors (http://www.realoakfloors.co.uk) offers the following advice: 'First, you need to know if your floor is oiled or lacquered (varnished). Have a close look – is there a sheen or a "layer" of varnish on it? If so, it will be lacquered. If, on the other hand, you can feel all the grain of the wood and it is very matt, the floor will be oiled – which is the case in 99% of all floors. Oiled floors need treating with maintenance oil around once a year. This generally involves putting a thin layer of oil on the floor and leaving it to dry for eight hours. For routine cleaning of oiled floors, use a pH-neutral cleaner such as Bona Kemi Carls Cleaner (around £6.00/$9.72 from Real Oak Floors, as before). Bona Kemi also makes freshen-up products for periodical cleaning, to get rid of any scuff marks, and a polish that will cover any scratches. There are several specialist cleaners for varnished floors: try HG Parquet Wooden Floor Cleaner/Polish (around £15.50/$25.11 http://www.diytools.co.uk).

The headrest of our Victorian armchair has bad grease stains. The cover is fitted silk so we can't put a cloth under the fabric to treat it. The stuffing is (we think) horsehair. How do we clean this? Help!

This is one for a professional cleaner I should think. Cleaning any horsehair-stuffed furniture is tricky because if you're not careful it can end up smelling awful. The National Carpet Cleaners' Association (http://www.ncca.co.uk/) is the only nationally recognised trade association dedicated to the cleaning of carpets and soft furnishings. They point out it that if the wrong chemical is used on the silk, or if the fabric is too wet, the horsehair may also release colour, which could then penetrate through to the surface. Natural body oils within the stained area are another consideration. They may have permanently affected the dyes within the fabric and weakened the silk, and would need to be dealt with depending on the severity. The NCCA will give you a list of approved companies in your area. They'll be able to assess the damage and may be able to improve it considerably.

I spilt a glass of water on my seagrass matting. I cleaned it up but the water soaked in and has left a brown stain. Help!

Although seagrass is naturally stain resistant, it doesn't react well to large quantities of liquid spillage. If you don't dry the damp patch immediately mould and mildew can form. Dab at the stain, working from the edges to the centre, using soap and water. If this doesn't work, Crucial Trading sells a care and cleaning box including a spot cleaner and brush specifically developed for natural floorings but it warns that mildew may be impossible to remove. (Around £40.00/$64.80 http://www.crucial-trading.com)

I am replacing some screws and ironmongery in my old Georgian house. How can I get them to match the 200 year old tarnished brass that's already there? Can the patination process be speeded up in any way? Help!

Antiquing Fluid is a patination fluid for ageing brass, copper and bronze, available in black, bronze or brown (around £10.00/$16.19 http://www.tryrelics.co.uk).

The Victorian hardware store Arkwrights, part of Cox's Architectural Salvage sells Liberon's Haematite brass, copper and bronze antiquing solution (Around £22.50/$36.45) which instantly ages unlacquered brass, copper and bronze fittings. There's also a version for iron and steel. (http://www.coxsarchitectural.co.uk)

I've tried various polishes on my old Liberty arts and crafts pewter coffee set without success. Help!

Richard Abdy, a liveryman of the Worshipful Company of Pewterers, which has been in existence since 1348 told me the way to clean pewter is to wash the pieces in soap and water and, after drying thoroughly, use a silver polish such as Silvo (around £2.50/$4.05 from supermarkets or hardware stores). Or try Soda Crystals. Soda Crystals are caustic so don't let any drip on waxed floors or it will strip the surface layer. Old pewter is a metal alloy of tin, copper and lead and should never be used for food or drink. There's no lead in modern pewter.

I blew out a candle and have got splatters of red candlewax all over the wall. It's covered in lining paper and painted with a matt emulsion. I've tried picking it off but it leaves a pink scratched pattern behind. Help!

Aim a hot hairdryer at the stains and, with a kitchen towel or absorbent cloth, dab off the wax as it melts. Be sure to hold the cloth to the wall underneath the wax as you melt it so that you catch any dribbles. Be careful not to hold the hairdryer too close to the wall or you may end up with burn marks on the fine lining paper. Another method is to place a sheet of brown wrapping paper over the wax and heat it with an electric iron through a towel. The wax is then absorbed into the paper. That said, this is probably the trickier option because of the increased possibility of burning. If any waxy stains remain on the wall, dip some damp cotton wool or a wet cotton bud in some baking powder (bicarbonate of soda) and gently dab at the stains. If your walls were painted with gloss or vinyl silk, you could use vinegar or white spirit instead of the bicarb.

Is there a cleaner that's safe to use on velvet upholstery? Help!

If there's no care label, start with the gentlest method, but test any application on a hidden seam, and vacuum well: with a damp E-cloth or soft hairbrush dampened in soda water, brush over the pile. If it's very dirty, add a scoop of oxygen bleach (widely available from supermarkets) to five litres of hot water. When dissolved, decant into a spray bottle, lightly mist the velvet, and brush with a soft brush dipped in soda water.

If the covers are removable and washable, turn inside out to protect the pile. To dry without creasing, hang in a steamy bathroom. If you need to iron, do so on the reverse, and use a towel as a base.

How clean are clothes washed at 30C (86F) or lower? Should we wash towels or underwear at higher temperatures? Help!

Clothes washed at 30C (86F) and below will come out clean, but dust mites, pet allergens, mould spores, pollen and bacteria will be completely removed only by heat – ie, at 60C (140F) plus. Mix a paste of detergent or oxygen bleach powder with a little water and apply to any stains before laundering. Detergent manufacturers recommend a hot machine maintenance wash once a month using a detergent that contains bleach.

My wooden chopping board has gone black at the edges where it's stood on damp surfaces. How can I clean it, ideally in an eco-friendly way? Help!

Use a nylon scourer and scrub with coarse salt and vinegar. If that doesn't work, 3% hydrogen peroxide (about £1 from pharmacy) is a strong, non-toxic bleaching agent that kills mould and lightens the stains it leaves behind – saturate the stains, leave for 15 minutes, then scrub with white vinegar. Borax is another natural mould-remover. Soaking wooden boards can warp them and open up the grain, so make a thick paste of borax and warm water, apply to the edges, leave for 30 minutes, scrub, rinse and leave to dry. Then, with a dry kitchen towel, apply a "food grade" mineral oil such as walnut or almond (not olive, cooking or vegetable). If none of this works, they're probably water marks, not mould, and the only way to remove those is to plane off the edges.

How do we remove black and red Biro marks from light oak dining room furniture? It's solid oak and oak veneer – Help!

Add a few drops of vinegar to a small bowl of milk to sour it. Soak a kitchen towel in the milk, cover the marks and place a weight – something like a vase or bowl – on top. Leave for 30 minutes, then rub. Repeat; repeat again, if necessary. The process can be speeded up by rubbing the marks with a little non-gel toothpaste between soakings. Toothpaste can lighten some woods and, if used too vigorously, damage veneer, so test first on a hidden, underpart of the table.

A friend has spilled foundation on my new cream carpet. As you can imagine, I'm not best pleased. Help!

WD-40 (from hardware stores) works on oily stains. Colour test first on an inconspicuous area of the carpet. Spray on to a clean white cloth and blot at the stain – don't rub – working from the outside in. Next, dilute a drop of washing-up liquid in a cup of hot water and blot again. Rinse thoroughly. If this doesn't do the trick, soak a cloth in diluted 3% hydrogen peroxide solution (from pharmacy), one part to six parts water, colour test, then leave on the stain for several hours. Alternatively, buy some Goo Gone. (See Chapter 2 for product details.)

How can I get candle-wax stains off a white linen tablecloth? I've removed the wax, but the pink stains remain. Help!

If there isn't a 'no bleach' symbol on the care label

(a triangle with a big cross on it), fully dissolve a quarter-scoop of oxygen bleach powder into 100ml(3.38oz) of hot water and stir into a thick cream. Apply directly to the stain and leave for up to five minutes (no longer, else the fabric may be permanently discoloured). Rinse thoroughly and launder using biological detergent. Air dry (ie don't tumble dry). If any mark remains, dab with a clean white cloth dipped in methylated spirits. As a last resort, mix equal parts of methylated spirits and ammonia (one of the few times when you can mix ammonia with anything). Ammonia is poisonous, so follow all safety instructions, ventilate the room, wear a mask and make sure all children and pets are very far away.

Our wood decking needs cleaning. I've been recommended powdered oxygen bleach as it cleans well and is nontoxic. Where can I buy it in reasonable quantities in the UK? Help!

An excellent nontoxic choice. When sold in bulk, oxygen bleach goes under its chemical name, sodium percarbonate, and it's quite hard to find. The Irish company Mistral Cleaning Products (http://www.mistralie.co.uk) sells a wide range of environmentally friendly, biodegradable specialist chemicals, from ecofriendly drain cleaners to nontoxic carpet cleaners. Sodium percarbonate costs from £8.53/$13.82 50g to £64.53/$104.55 25kg. You probably want something in the middle range. The cost for 5kg is £31.74/$51.42.

I've spilled Danish oil on a window and it has dried hard. How can I get it off without scratching the glass? Help!

Soak a very fine-grade wire wool in methylated spirits or turps, and rub gently over the marks. Failing that, try a solvent varnish remover. Nitromors All-Purpose Paint & Varnish Remover (around £7.00/$11.34 from hardware stores) is a powerful paint and varnish stripper particularly suitable for vertical surfaces. Wearing goggles and gloves, dab on a thick coat by brush. Wait for the varnish to blister, apply another coat, working it well into the blisters, and leave for 20 minutes without letting it dry out. Skim off with a scraper knife. If the varnish doesn't come away easily, apply more solvent. Wash with liquid detergent in cold water and follow council guidelines for the disposal of empty containers. If that sounds too scary, De-Solv-It's Contractors Solvent (from hardware stores, or around £5.00/$8.10 from B&Q) may work. It removes oils and grease, etc, from glass: again, follow safety instructions.

I have a Dyson 01 upright vacuum cleaner. The brush is clogged with fluff after being used for a year on a new fitted carpet. I can't remove the brush, and the fluff feels sticky and resistant to removal. Help!

I contacted Dyson who said, "First ensure your cleaner is switched off, then turn it upside down. You should be able to see three silver screws that hold the soleplate in place. If you undo the screws, you'll have clear access to the brush bar to remove the fluff." For more information, contact Dyson. I would add that if the fluff is too congealed to pull away easily, loosen by spraying with a little WD-40. Wash off the WD-40 with washing-up liquid and rinse well before replacing.

I've just bought a vintage bedstead from eBay

and, unfortunately, the mahogany headboard smells of stale smoke. How do I get rid of the odour?

Wipe down the wood with neat white vinegar, then dust with bicarbonate of soda and leave for a few hours. Or go straight in with borax. Dissolve 2 cups (700g) of borax in two litres of hot water. If wiping over doesn't do the trick, sprinkle borax powder over the damp headboard or soak old towels in the solution and wrap around the headboard, keeping them there until dry. Failing that, add ammonia (half a cup/125ml ammonia: two litres of water/borax solution), but follow the safety instructions and rinse well as ammonia fumes are poisonous.

I splashed toothpaste on my Moroccan leather slippers and it left a dark mark. I bought some leather upholstery cleaner, but it left a light patch. Help!

Dab the mark with a solution of equal parts white vinegar and water. If that doesn't work, make a paste of lemon juice and cream of tartar, apply to the stain, leave for a few hours, then wipe off with a damp cloth. You may have used the type of leather cleaner that lifts the dye as well as the dirt. Leather recolouring balm (around £15.00/$24.30 from http://furnitureclinic.co.uk) restores the colour, but it only works if it can soak into the leather. Test with a drop of water on the mark and see if it soaks in. If the leather isn't absorbent, try Furniture Clinic's leather repair touch-up kit (around £25.00/$40.50).

What is the best way to deal with mildew on my Laura Ashley lined curtains? They're meant to be dry clean only, but the cleaner says this will kill the

mildew but not get rid of the stains. Help!

First brush off what you can. Do this outside, so the spores don't spread. Next, foam up some biological detergent in lukewarm water and, using just the foam, wipe over the mould. Rinse with a sponge dampened in white vinegar. If that doesn't work, mix a teaspoon of tea tree oil in a cup of lukewarm water and spray over. Shake between each spray to ensure the oil is evenly distributed. Try a top-quality Australian oil such as Jason Organic Tea Tree Oil (around £12.00/$19.44 http://www.lucyrose.biz), which has concentrated fungi-busting powers.

How can I stop my cotton pillowcases from turning yellow? I wash them at 30-40C (86-104F), using nonbio powder, and dry them naturally indoors in winter and outdoors in summer. Help!

To remove the yellowing, soak overnight in a strong solution of soda crystals dissolved at a ratio of one cup: one pint hot water. Or use borax or Dylon Fabric Power Whitener (from hardware stores, or about £2.00/$3.24 from fredaldous.co.uk). Then launder at the hottest temperature the fabric can take. Nonbio detergents contain bleaching agents, but as a booster for regular low-temperature washing, add a scoop of oxygen bleach and half a cup of soda crystals (or borax). Add half a cup of vinegar to the conditioner drawer as a fabric softener.

I have a candlewax figurine that has a film of dust and dirt on it. How best to clean it?

Try a nylon stocking sprayed with a glass cleaner such as Windolene (around £1.00/$1.62, from supermarkets). If that doesn't get off all the dirt, isopropyl, or 'rubbing' alcohol, will. It's poisonous and very flammable, so follow instructions. Not many pharmacies stock it, but you can find it on eBay for around £5.00/$8.10. That said, isopropyl alcohol is a constituent part of Dettol, so try that first.

We've just returned from Marrakech with a lovely red leather pouffe. Unfortunately, a strong camel smell emanates from it. Help!

If the leather's textured rather than shiny, bicarbonate of soda might do it. Give it a good dusting, dampen with a water mist sprayer and leave the soda on for a few days, topping up and dampening every so often, before brushing off. Alternatively, wrap the pouffe in cloths soaked in ammonia and put in a bin-liner overnight (follow safety instructions, don't inhale, rinse thoroughly) or use a car upholstery odour remover – Fitzgerald's Odor Fogger is a powerful US product used by the professionals (around £7.00/$11.34 on ebay.co.uk).

I occasionally see silverfish in a cupboard in my bathroom. Are these creatures dirty? And how do I get rid of them?

Silverfish aren't dirty, but indicative of damp. They thrive in dark, damp conditions and feed on the glue that sticks together cardboard containers, fabric and books, which is how they (or their eggs) got into your cupboard. Removing such temptations isn't going to help much, because silverfish can last a year between meals. Scattering cloves and dusting the cracks in your cupboard with salt or borax might work, but your best bet is Diatomaceous Earth, an easily powdered rock that sucks the liquids from their skin, causing them to dehydrate and die. It also gets rid of fleas and other insects (Around £6.00/$9.72 from Wiggly Wigglers).

My teak garden table spent the winter outside uncovered and now has lichen-like growth on the top. How do I remove and clean it? Help!

Sodium percarbonate (pure oxygen bleach, from http://www.mistralie.co.uk) releases oxygen through the formation of hydrogen peroxide, which pierces the cell walls of fungi, bacteria, moss, lichen, etc and destroys the cells. Dissolve 70-80g (one third of a cup) in warm/hot water, apply to the surface and leave for 30 minutes to one hour. Agitate with a soft brush and rinse well. The solution will remain active for five to six hours, after which it should be discarded. Unused material may be poured down the drain or into a septic tank. It's nontoxic and non-polluting. Don't be tempted to use solvent wood cleaners such as oxalic acid and trisodium phosphate, because these can discolour teak.

My house has a polished oak parquet floor in excellent condition. However, its beauty is spoiled by a water stain. How can I get rid of it? Help!

I asked wood floor experts Flooring First, who suggested sanding and applying a wood stain of the same colour over the top. Because different woods take stain differently, this can be tricky. However, as your stain is relatively small, you might get away with it. Top-quality staining products are made by Bona, Osmo and Morrells – contact Flooring Centre Wood Flooring Supplies for details. Stainers should be applied along the length of each floor block. Don't apply more than one layer, or the colour won't remain even. Alternatively, to have a 14 sq m (150 sq ft) floor professionally stripped and revarnished would cost around £320.00/$518.48.

I think we have bed bugs. I have a sealed hypoallergic mattress cover – how have they got in? Do I take off the cover to look for them? Help!

Bedbugs are nasty flat, brown insects that come out at night to feed on your blood. The telltale sign is itching at night, but not everybody is affected; the other big clue is red blood spots on your sheets and pillows. The bugs are most commonly found nesting in wood – bed frames usually, as they like to be near their source of food (you), but they can also get into wardrobes, drawers, skirting boards, clothing, curtain seams and more. Look for clusters of black dots (the faeces) and smaller white dots (the eggs). Home sprays won't work – call your council pest control service, which will spray all the wood in your room with a toxic chemical. This will cost around £100.00/$162.00. You'll have to clear out cupboards, under-bed storage etc. The chemical takes several weeks to work. Don't move anything out of the room that isn't sealed in a plastic bag or the bugs could spread. If you're itching, don't move elsewhere in the night. Move to a different room the next day until the bugs have been eradicated.

My granddaughter has decorated my favourite brown cotton quilt with her bright yellow nappy rash ointment. I've tried hot soapy water, neat washing-up liquid, Vanish, but I can't get rid of the whitish residue. Help!

"You need a powerful stain remover that works well on greasy marks. Which? has just tested some and Ecover Ecological Stain Remover Liquid (around

£3.00/$4.86)) scored very highly, coming second and receiving a special mention for its removal of grease stains. Or try a non-greasy make-up remover such as Body Shop's Camomile Gentle Eye Make-Up Remover (around £3.00/$4.86). As a last resort, mix bicarbonate of soda with water and leave on the stain for a couple of hours – not the best solution because bicarb can lift colour and damage some fabrics. Always do a colour test on a hidden seam first.

Is there a toilet descaler that actually works? I must have tried every one on the market, but they are about as effective as tap water. Help!

Empty out the water first (use a disposable cup), then leave a neat concentrate to dwell on the surface for a bit before scrubbing off. Remove light build-ups by placing kitchen towels soaked in vinegar or lemon juice over the stains and leaving overnight. For heavier marks, use a safe, concentrated formula such as Eco Blast (around £6.00/$9.72 from bionetix.co.uk), a powerful low pH cleaner made from natural ingredients that is non-corrosive (important if you're using it as a poultice). To avoid future build-up, spray regularly with vinegar, or place an Ecozone Magnoloo Toilet Descaler in the cistern (around £10.00/$16.20 from http://www.johnlewis.com). Never mix toilet cleaners – they may react, creating dangerous, toxic gas.

I make a lot of jam. Neighbours give me jars, but it takes endless soaking and scraping to get the labels off. Help!

My jam-making friend has the same problem. There's always a white film left. But you can now get removers in a gel that clings to vertical surfaces, so can be left to soak in. Try Lakeland's Sticky Stuff Remover Gel Kit (around £4.50/$7.29) or De.solv.it Sticky Stuff Remover Gel (around £4.50/$7.29 from B&Q). Alternatively, soak overnight in a strong soda crystal solution (1 cup to 2 cups hot water).

We have a dining table covered in a thin veneer. I stained it a dark oak to go with the rest of the furniture and over time it has become sticky. I have lightly sanded, re-stained and varnished it, but the stickiness is still apparent.

I asked Mark Baker of the Guild of Master Craftsmen's Woodworking magazine. "You need to know about the piece, its value, finish etc, before starting such ventures," he says. "Some dyes/stains should be applied only to bare wood. When you sanded it down, the wood might not have been taken right back to its original state so the stain may not have been able to fully cure/dry. This means the varnish can never set and will remain sticky. Some water-based varnishes can become sticky when used on tables if hot plates, or oils from salads, aren't cleaned off quickly." Fill out the contact form at http://www.woodworkersinstitute.com and Mark can advise you further.

A toddler got her hands on a black permanent marker and scribbled on my cream linen sofa and coffee table. I removed the marker from the table with a baby wipe, but I can't shift the sofa stain.

Check the fabric label to see if it's dry clean-only and/or Scotchgard-protected – like dry clean-only, that needs a solvent-based remover. Check the pen label and visit the manufacturer's website to see what it recommends. Methylated spirits may work. Apply with an absorbent, clean white cloth in small amounts, 'feathering' from the outside in, so you don't spread the mark. For old, dried-in marks, try acetone (nail polish remover). As a last resort, mix meths with ammonia 50/50.

My cotton bedspread, crocheted by my grandmother, has iron rust spots. How do I remove them? Help!

Soak them in white vinegar for 30 minutes or rub with half a lemon sprinkled with salt, then rinse. If these don't work, make a paste of lemon juice and cream of tartar, colour-test on a hidden seam, and if OK leave on for 15 minutes. Rinse well. Or make a paste of cream of tartar and 3% hydrogen peroxide solution. Test for 15 minutes maximum. If it lightens the test seam, make a new paste of hydrogen peroxide solution diluted 50:50 with water and re-test. If OK, apply to stains. Leave for 15 minutes maximum. Rinse and wash at low temperature. Don't tumble dry until all the marks have gone.

I have a 30s Royal Doulton ceramic bathroom sink on a deco pewter-coloured stand. How do I clean both? Help!

A general-purpose cleaner will work fine on the sink. A powder like Barkeepers Friend (from supermarkets) can also be used in concentrated form to shift heavy stains. Bicarbonate of soda is another gentle but effective cleaner. For general daily wiping of the sink and for the base use an E-Cloth (around £4.99/$8.08). It lasts for years and will also quickly polish taps, chrome fittings, towel rails, windows and mirrors.

My silver cutlery, which dates from the 1920s, is

looking a bit of a mess. Can it be replated? Help!

Find a metals conservator. At the Institute of Conservation's Register, (http://www.icon.org.uk) select your postal area, then, under the 'Specialisms' field, highlight 'metalwork, object'. Most give an idea of cost (from £30/$48.60 an hour) and recent work. The site also has guidelines on storage and maintenance.

I've spilled candle wax all over a thick cotton table runner. How do I remove it? Help!

Harden the wax by putting a bag of ice on top or by putting the runner in a plastic bag and into the freezer. Then just pick off the hardened wax. Or lay brown wrapping paper over the wax and heat it with an electric iron through a towel – the paper absorbs the wax. This is a trickier option because of the risk of burning, and you'll also be left with a greasy stain and, if it's a coloured candle, possibly a dye stain. Clear up the greasy residue with neat washing-up liquid and rinse well. If that doesn't work, put WD-40 (or methylated spirits) on a white absorbent cloth and dab it with that, then clean off with washing-up liquid and rinse thoroughly. If there are any dye stains, make a paste of biological washing powder, leave over the stain for 30 minutes or so, then rinse. Failing that, try a paste of oxygen bleach, though colour test first.

We recently bought a five-year-old home that has never been lived in. Whenever we mop the baths, a fishy smell lingers for hours. Help!

I checked with my plumber who advises: "Because your home was empty for so long, the water in the trap seals may have evaporated. If you're only mopping, and not using the baths, not enough water will have accumulated in the u-bend to stop smells coming up from the sewers. Shallow baths of water emptied in one go should restore the seals." Melting plastic around faulty electrics can give off a fishy smell, so if it turns out to not be the seals, call an electrician urgently.

After a birthday meal on an oak wood block dining table, we lifted an iron candlestick and found a black ring underneath. We've tried every cleaner. Help!

As the cleaners haven't worked, a light sanding would be the next step. A last resort would be oxalic acid, which removes dark iron stains and works well on oak. It's dangerous stuff, though, and will probably lighten the wood more than you want. You'd then have to restain the wood to match the original. All best left to the professionals. If you're confident at DIY, Construction Chemicals sells an Oxalic Acid Safety Kit (around £32.00/$51.84), which comes with goggles, gloves, instructions and a phone helpline. If you have a good accidental damage clause in your home contents insurance, you could claim for a professional repair, or even a replacement table.

LINKS

Architectural Salvage, Reclaimed Building Materials, Recycling

Cox's Architectural www.coxsarchitectural.co.uk

Salvo www.salvo.co.uk

Reduce Reuse Recycle www.reducereuserecycle.co.uk

Antique restoration, finishing & paint supplies
www.tryrelics.co.uk

Bath & Beauty

Antipodes Organic www.beautybazaar.co.uk

About Animal Testing www.aboutanimaltesting.co.uk

Weleda www.weleda.co.uk

Antipodes Organic www.skincarebeautyproducts.co.uk

Honesty Cosmetics www.honestycosmetics.co.uk

Safe Cosmetics www.safecosmetics.co.uk

Campaign for safe cosmetics www.safecosmetics.org

There Must Be A Better Way
www.theremustbeabetterway.co.uk

Red 23 www.red23.co.uk

Vit Shop www.vit-shop.co.uk

Body Ecology www.bodyecology.com

Good Guide www.goodguide.com

Cosmetics Database www.cosmeticsdatabase.com

Organic grocery & body care
www.oliverswholefoods.co.uk

Bodykind www.bodykind.com

Consumer Advice

Independent advice www.moneysavingexpert.com

The Energy Saving Trust
www.energysavingtrust.org.uk

153

Supermarket Offers Comparison UK
www.mysupermarket.co.uk
Name, shame and claim www.canyoutrustthem.com

DIY & White Goods

Independent advice, spare parts, forums
www.ukwhitegoods.co.uk
Construction Chemicals
www.constructionchemicals.co.uk
Tool Mix www.toolmix.com
Ecos Paints www.ecospaints.com
Electrical spares & accessories www.partmaster.co.uk
Conserv Stone Restoration specialist
www.lime-mortars.co.uk
Pure Adhesion (for Lithofin)
www.pureadhesion.co.uk
Tikko products www.tikkoproducts.co.uk
Stainless steel www.ulti-met.co.uk
Heritage Home & Garden
www.heritage-homeandgarden.co.uk
Anti-slipping www.slipsolve.com
Chandlery World www.chandleryworld.co.uk
Grout Protection www.groutprotection.co.uk
Briwax dye touch-up pen www.briwaxwoodcare.com
Sinks-Taps www.sinks-taps.com

Environment

UK Health & Safety Executive information on
REACH www.hse.gov.uk/REACH
Greenpeace www.greenpeace.org.uk
Friends of the Earth www.foe.co.uk
My Zero Waste www.myzerowaste.com
The Good Human www.thegoodhuman.com
Green Living Tips www.greenlivingtips.com
The Health and Environment Alliance

www.env-health.org

The Chemicals Health Monitor Project
www.chemicalshealthmonitor.org

Chem Sec (International Chemical Sectariat)
www.chemsec.org

US Environmental Protection Agency's Introduction to Indoor Air Quality www.epa.gov/iaq/ia-intro.html

378 Substances of Very High Concern www.sinlist.org

REACH
www.ec.europa.eu/environment/chemicals/reach/reach_intro.htm

Chem Trust www.chemtrust.org.uk

Safer Houses www.saferhouses.co.uk

US The Greenest Dollar www.thegreenestdollar.com

US Good Guide www.goodguide.com

US Safer Chemicals, Healthy Families
www.saferchemicals.org

US Women's Voice For The Earth
www.womensvoices.org

Find a Specialist

Antiques in all fields www.conservationregister.com

Guild of Master Craftsmen www.findacraftsman.com

Glass and Glazing Federation www.ggf.co.uk

The National Carpet Cleaners' Association
www.ncca.co.uk

Institute of Vitreous Enamellers and Vitreous Enamel

Association www.ive.org.uk

British Antique Furniture Restorers' Assoc
http://www.bafra.org.uk/index.html

British Stainless Steel Association www.bssa.org.uk

Yell UK business directory www.yell.com

Find a reliable, trustworthy tradesman
www.trustmark.org.uk

Floors

Natural wooden flooring www.wood-you-like.co.uk

All types of flooring helpline
www.completelyflooring.co.uk

Stone floors www.stonefloorsdirect.co.uk

Natural floorcoverings
www.naturalrugstore.co.uk www.crucial-trading.com

National Carpet Cleaners Association
www.ncca.co.uk

Rubber floors www.therubberflooringcompany.co.uk

Oriental rugs www.hillcorugs.com

Real oak floors www.realoakfloors.co.uk

Solid wood & natural flooring
www.urbaneliving.co.uk

Health and Diet

Maggie's Cancer Caring Centre
www.maggiescentres.org

The World Cancer Research Fund www.wcrf-uk.org

No More BPA Campaign www.nomorebpa.org.uk

Cancer Research UK www.cancerresearchuk.org

US Consumer Guide The Daily Green
www.thedailygreen.com

US Seventh Generation www.seventhgeneration.com

Ecover www.ecover.com

Canadian Medical Association www.cma.ca

About.com Urban Legends
www.urbanlegends.about.com

London herbalist www.holisticherbal.co.uk

Cancer Active www.canceractive.com

Household Cleaning

E-cloth ® www.e-cloth.com

Vinegar Institute www.versatilevinegar.org

WD-40 fan club www.fanclub.wd40.com/
Natural Collection www.naturalcollection.com
Mistral www.mistralie.co.uk
Chemist Direct www.chemistdirect.co.uk
Decorating Direct www.decoratingdirect.co.uk
Green Store Online www.thegreenstoreonline.com
Lakeland www.lakeland.co.uk
Axminster www.axminster.co.uk
Partridges www.partridges.co.uk
Quickleen www.quickleen.co.uk
Ocado www.ocado.com
Toolastic www.tooltastic.com
Lawson Shop www.lawsonshop.co.uk
Plumb World www.plumbworld.co.uk
Housemakers www.housemakers.co.uk
Ethical Consumer (US) www.ethicalconsumer.org

Paint

Ecos Paints www.ecospaints.com
Earthborn Paints www.earthbornpaints.co.uk
Urbane Living www.urbaneliving.co.uk

Public Health

US Environmental Protection Agency www.epa.gov
The Environment Agency Drinking Water
Inspectorate
   www.dwi.gov.uk
Chemicals Health Monitor
www.chemicalshealthmonitor.org
Water analysis www.acornwater.com
Consumer Council for Water www.ccwater.org.uk
International Association for Soaps, Detergents and
Maintenance Products www.aise.eu

Tiles

Tile doctor www.tiledoctor.co.uk
Tilestone Solutions www.tilestonesolutions.co.uk
The Natural Tile Studio www.thenaturaltilestudio.com

Misc

Make It And Mend It www.makeitandmendit.com

The Fly Lady www.flylady.net

Pest Stop www.pest-stop.co.uk

Pest control supplies www.diypcs.co.uk

Primrose London garden centre & pest control www.primrose-london.co.uk

The Electric Blanket Institute (USA) www.electricblanketinstitute.com

Ercol www.furniturerestorationuk.com

Dog & Cat Nappies www.dog-nappy.co.uk

Odour beaters www.kennelsupplies.co.uk

Pure Silk Duvets www.puresilkduvet.com

Sulis silks (for specialist silk cleaner) www.sulis.co.uk

Aquarium stores (for activated carbon air freshener) www.aquaessentials.co.uk; www.swelluk.com

Ethical Superstore www.ethicalsuperstore.com

Rayburn www.rayburn-web.co.uk

Le Creuset www.lecreuset.co.uk

Leather furniture care www.furnitureclinic.co.uk www.springvaleleather.co.uk

Bird Shit Remover www.birdshitremover.co.uk

Air Sterilisers www.airsterilisers.co.uk

Cutlery www.thedinersclub.co.uk

Leather restoration www.mlworkshop.co.uk

Duvet restuffing & restoration www.thefeathercompany.com

Car valet & Aromatek smell busters www.euroshine.co.uk

Scratched glass repair www.scratchglass.com

John Lewis www.johnlewis.com
Ryman www.ryman.co.uk
Jerry's Artarama (US) www.jerrysartarama.com
Greetings Cards and gifts http://www.moonpig.com
Postcards by email http://postcard.com
Paw Mark www.pawmark.co.uk
Green Pan www.green-pan.com

ACKNOWLEDGEMENTS

My grateful thanks to Dr Anne Steinemann for permission to quote from her letter about the dangers of air fresheners and to Professor Philippa Darbre for filling me in on her latest work on parabens and breast cancer. Thanks to Michael Macintyre for his forensic proof reading, Emma Boden for her contributing edit and pitch-perfect publicity and Jennifer Copley-May for her fabulous logo artwork. Also to Sarah Tomley at Hamlyn for commissioning my first stains book and to Hannah Booth, my editor at The Guardian, for feeding me a constant supply of readers' dilemmas to solve. To Nadia Brydon for her fab smoothie course at the Fulham Breast Cancer Haven, to Kathryn, Rachel, Monique, Lorna and all at Maggie's Cancer Caring Centre, London who have helped me so very much in so many ways over a very difficult period of caring for somebody with cancer.

10% of all profits from this book will be donated to Maggie's in memory of my amazing cousin Jennie Trisnan. Jennie knew very well how a good diet and emotional care could help prolong lives. She was way ahead of her time and helped so many to do so before she died.

More NonFiction by Stephanie Zia

Stain Removal: Your Really Useful Guide to Getting Rid of Stains (Hamlyn 2005)
The Easy No-Nonsense Guide to Stain Removal (Make it and Mend it 2009)
Baby Names Inspiring Names for Every Day of the Year (Hamlyn 2005)
The Decontamination Bible (Sweet Fennel, Taiwan)

About The Author

Stephanie was a BBC-TV production assistant, researcher and director before leaving to become a full-time mum and writer. Author of 2 Piatkus commercial fiction novels and 2 Hamlyn non-fiction books, from 2005–11 she was the cleaning guru for *The Guardian* newspaper's popular *Space Solves* column. Stephanie enjoys editing and producing other authors' titles at Blackbird Digital Books. She lives in London.

www.blackbird-books.com
LONDON

blackbird
blackbird-books.com

Printed in Poland
by Amazon Fulfillment
Poland Sp. z o.o., Wrocław